Persistent Petty Offenders

90 0708822 1

KW-491-928

By Suz airhead

PLYMOUTH POLYTECHNIC
LIBRARY

Accn. No.	
Class. No.	
Contl. No.	

A HOME OFFICE
RESEARCH UNIT
REPORT

LONDON: HER MAJESTY'S STATIONERY OFFICE

© *Crown copyright 1981*
First published 1981

HOME OFFICE RESEARCH STUDIES

'Home Office Research Studies' comprise reports on research undertaken in the Home Office to assist in the exercise of its administrative functions, and for the information of the judicature, the services for which the Home Secretary has responsibility (direct or indirect) and the general public.

On the last pages of this report are listed titles already published in this series, and in the preceding series *Studies in the Causes of Delinquency and the Treatment of Offenders.*

PLYMOUTH POLYTECHNIC LIBRARY	
Accn. No.	126235-0
Class. No.	364.37 FAI
Contl. No.	0 11 340 7068

ISBN 0 11 340706 8

Foreword

WITHDRAWN FROM UNIVERSITY OF PLYMOUTH LIBRARY SERVICES

The problem of the persistent petty offender is not a new one; it has been of concern, in various guises, for a century or more. In so far as the problem is identified with vagrancy, its history goes back at least to the sixteenth century. At the present time, the increase in the size of the prison population and consequent overcrowding has brought up the question of whether persistent petty offenders need be in prison and indeed whether they should be kept out of the criminal justice system altogether.

This volume reports the results of research which had as its starting point persistent petty offenders in Pentonville and then turned its attention to their arrest, sentencing and eventual discharge from prison. The final chapter explores measures to alleviate the problem in so far as it affects the criminal justice system.

I J CROFT
Head of the Research Unit

September 1980

Acknowledgements

Thanks are due to the many people who were involved in these studies.

I am indebted to the Governor of Pentonville Prison and to his staff, especially those in the welfare liaison unit; to officers in the Metropolitan Police and the Sussex Police; to members of the Magistrates' Association and to the magistrates, clerks to the justices and probation officers in Birmingham, Coventry and Oxford. I am particularly grateful to Mr S Gilbert who ran the action project in Pentonville, and to Elaine Busby who, during an assignment to the Home Office Research Unit as a sandwich student, undertook fieldwork and data analysis.

Chapter six of this report, about the socially isolated prisoners' project, has been contributed by John Corden and Maggie Clifton of the University of York.

SUZAN FAIRHEAD

Contents

1 Introduction

Defining the target group

This research was the consequence of a concern to reduce the size of the prison population in order to relieve overcrowding, particularly of the local prisons. Various strategies could be adopted to achieve this, for example awarding shorter sentences to all those imprisoned, increasing remission or granting more people parole. The method investigated here, however, constituted an attempt to identify a section of the prison population that might be kept out of custody altogether. Two questions required to be answered: which group(s) could reasonably be removed? and what extra facilities would need to be provided elsewhere?

The level of overcrowding is already such that the savings would have to be fairly substantial. This could be achieved by removing a large number of persons who spend short periods in prison or a small number who spend long periods there. The first course would spread the load of diversion widely, possibly requiring the injection of resources on a large scale with disproportionately little effect on the prison population. Of those individuals who spend a good part of their lives in prison, there are two distinct types: those receiving long sentences for serious offences and those sentenced at frequent intervals to short spells of imprisonment for less serious offences, namely *persistent* offenders.

The diversion of any group from prison has to be comparable firstly with public notions of acceptability and, therefore, must have regard to the safety of the community. Secondly, although sentencing properly takes account of an individual history and circumstances, the need for justice dictates that more serious offences attract harsher penalties. In view of both of these criteria the most readily divertible offenders are those who have committed fairly trivial offences, namely *petty* offenders.

The definition formulated for the group to be kept out of prison combined the two criteria of persistent and petty offending. This is a heterogeneous group but certain social characteristics appear to be common. For example, as evident from the survey of persistent petty offenders in Pentonville described in Chapter 2, homelessness and poverty are widespread. These factors seem to be directly associated with persistent petty offending in that some individuals currently face much worse penalties for their behaviour than do others because of their circumstances. In the vast majority of cases when a person appears for drunkenness the penalty is a fine. This represents no problem for the person who has

1

means to pay but is one for the person living at or below subsistence level. Moreover the magistrates are empowered to send forthwith to prison those of no fixed address who lack the funds to pay immediately. To take another example, a well-dressed person observed to be asking for money for a bus fare is unlikely to be arrested for begging, whereas a down-and-out doing the same runs a far greater risk. Through appropriate intervention it may be possible to reduce the incidence of individuals being arrested and imprisoned largely as a result of the disadvantages they experience.

Age appears a relevant factor in deciding which offenders to keep out of prison. It is apparent from previous studies (eg Banks and Fairhead, 1976), as well as the research reported in this volume, that the incidence and severity of disadvantage, such as homelessness and isolation from family and friends, are greater among older offenders. Moreover, in the case of younger offenders there remains some optimism that individuals can change, or be changed, and thus find an escape route from the penal revolving door syndrome, whereby they appear again and again in the courts and return again and again to prison. However, the glimmer of hope fades as individuals grow older and the main consideration, when planning alternatives to current decisions, becomes how to maintain them in ways that are less costly or more humane.

The tag 'persistent petty offender' is difficult to translate into precise operational terms. To be a 'persistent' offender depends on being apprehended and being processed by the criminal justice system. In general the more visible the individual, the more likely he is to be caught for offending and the homeless tend to be visible because they have to spend their time in public places by virtue of having nowhere else to go. However, there is some evidence that there is an extreme group of homeless people who tend to be avoided by the police (and everyone else), because they are lice-ridden, dirty and smelly, and who therefore cease to get involved with the criminal justice system even though they continue to engage in behaviour for which others are arrested. Thus, persistence in terms of numbers of recorded convictions cannot be taken as a measure of persistence in actual offending. The homeless poor may be persistently taken to court, and hence persistently returned to prison, because of a persistent failure to provide for them in any other way.

Equally problematic is the definition of a 'petty' offence. Although some offences, notably drunkenness (except in connection with driving), begging and wandering abroad are exceptions, pettiness cannot generally be categorised simply in terms of type of offence. By and large a non-indictable offence will be petty, but although some indictable offences can obviously be ruled out (murder, grievous bodily harm, rape) the vast majority of them will be petty or not, according to their circumstances. In general a petty offence is one that does not cause much harm to any victim. Most categories of offences of sex and violence are thus excluded, but some incidents of indecent exposure and technical assaults, which result in no injury, can be seen as petty.

2

In general petty property offences are unlikely to involve large sums of money or objects of high value. They are likely to be opportunistic, determined by a situation which presents an easy opportunity, for example theft from a shop display or of articles left in an unlocked vehicle, and be to satisfy immediate needs (such as theft of food, drink or clothing, or breaking into an empty building as a place to sleep).

In their report, *The Petty Short-Term Prisoner*, Banks and Fairhead (1976) described the way in which they had selected petty offenders among those serving short-term sentences (ie 18 months or less) in a ten per cent stratified random sample of the population of prisons in the South-East region on a given date. The purpose was to identify those who, on the basis of their entire criminal career could be classified as petty offenders. To do this, up to four researchers read through each criminal history containing the fullest available description of every offence, and a very high level of inter-rater agreement was found not only about the classification of single offences but also about records spanning many years.

After the subjective exercise was completed a discriminant analysis showed that the characteristic that best distinguished petty offenders from the rest in the sample was the length of sentence being served, the petty offenders being awarded shorter terms on average. A follow-up study on this sample indicated that it was very rare for a petty offender to commit an offence which took him out of this category in the subsequent two years. This suggests that offenders who have established a pattern of trivial offences are unlikely to become suddenly a greater menace to the community.

Apart from these operational difficulties in using the label 'petty persistent offenders', it also needs to be used in a flexible way according to context. While the underlying principle of the definition remained the same over all the research exercises (ie focussing on a group which could, without detriment to public safety or to justice, be dealt with by means which reduced involvement with the criminal justice system) the way the group was identified in practice varied from study to study according to which characteristics were salient for each. All the studies focussed on older individuals, and homelessness was always a funda-mental characteristic. With the obvious exception of research in Pentonville (a men's prison), both men and women were included. However, too few cases of women were encountered in the empirical work for reliable generalisations about them to be made.

Development of the research programme
The programme of research described in this report comprised four separate studies undertaken by the Home Office Research Unit and a fifth external one. The external project, described in Chapter 6, has a rather different background but is concerned with the same target group. The Research Unit studies developed from the common starting point that has been outlined above.

The first study, described in Chapter 2, was intended to describe the social disadvantage experienced by persistent petty offenders, especially to gain information from the individuals themselves about how their needs might be met. The definition of 'persistent petty' employed in this case was straight-forward. Persistent was gauged in terms of having a given number of previous convictions, and pettiness was defined mainly in terms of length of sentence. Three samples were selected. The main one was of men aged 30 and over sentenced to immediate imprisonment. The two additional samples were: one of men aged 30 and over in prison in default of paying fines and one of men under 30.

This initial study drew attention to the welfare needs which would have to be met if persistent petty offenders were to be diverted from prison, or from the criminal justice system altogether, but could not point to how diversion might be achieved. Three decision-making points were therefore studied: the point of arrest and charge by the police; the point of passing sentence in the magistrates' court; and the point of discharge from prison.

In the case of the action research project described in Chapter 5 the target group was defined in terms of the service offered. The descriptive study had indicated that accommodation was in some ways the key requirement among persistent petty offenders in Pentonville and also the one that could most easily be tackled. The placing project initiated in the welfare liaison unit there was thus designed to enable prisoners who were of no fixed abode when they were received into prison to be helped into better accommodation than they could probably find for themselves on release. It was aimed at those who had formerly not been afforded much welfare help, namely those serving short sentences. By virtue of their sentence length this group could be assumed to have committed trivial offences, and the vast majority of the prisoners included in the project had at least six previous convictions.

When the police take a decision about whether to arrest an offender they may have no knowledge of that individual's past record. However homelessness, found in the preliminary study to be highly associated with membership of the older group of persistent petty offenders, is relevant to them. Early in any encounter the police ask for an individual's name and address; having no address, or giving the address of a common lodging house or hostel, may affect the subsequent course of events. Therefore in the studies of police behaviour, described in Chapter 3, petty offending and being of no fixed abode were used to define the group under consideration.

Magistrates, however, have information about an individual's previous convictions and take this into account in deciding the sentence. They also take into account whether the person has a home, a job, a family, etc as secondary considerations. The instructions for the questionnaire survey in magistrates courts described in Chapter 4, asked for returns to be completed for individuals who had four or more previous convictions, at least one of which was within the past

4

18 months, who had committed a petty offence. Guidance was offered about which offences to include as 'petty' and attention was drawn to the problem of sentencing the homeless and those without a base in the community. An age limit was set for the questionnaire survey and only returns for those aged 25 or more were included in the analysis.

Estimating numbers for diversion

The choice of an operational definition of 'persistent petty offender' obviously directly affects the size of the group identified for potential diversion. The studies reported in this volume were all concerned with groups at the extreme of the spectrum in terms of triviality of offending. The main focus of the research was, moreover, on those who offend with much greater than average frequency. The size of the group that fits both of these criteria is therefore necessarily numerically small. The choice of cut off points, in terms of sentence length and number of previous convictions, however, not only affects the size of the group but also alters its homogeneity in terms of its requirements for alternative provision. As the cut off points become more exclusive, the average age of the group increases and the disadvantage experienced by them becomes more concentrated, a point which is illustrated using data from the South East prison population survey by Fairhead and Marshall (1979) in a paper delivered to a seminar organised by the National Association for the Care and Rehabilitation of Offenders (NACRO) on the subject of the persistent petty offender. A contribution by Barnard and Bottoms to the same seminar employed a much wider definition, encompassing younger offenders as well as older ones. Different strategies are, however, needed in order to divert this group, requiring primarily alternative ways of controlling and supervising them, and not always demanding the extra welfare provisions that seem necessary before the extreme group of older offenders can be successfully diverted.

Drawbacks of observational methods

The studies using observational methods, described in Chapters 3 and 4, presented the problem inherent in such an approach, that the presence of the researcher might alter the behaviour under study. The researcher attempted to minimise this by becoming 'part of the furniture' as far as was possible. However on occasion the researcher noted an obvious effect due to her presence on the action taken by both police and magistrates, which serves to emphasise the latitude of discretion they enjoy, but also means that the results must be treated with some caution if they seem to conflict with other evidence.

Further research

Although the research exercise described in Chapters 3–5 has been completed, the programme of action research into how to keep persistent petty offenders out of prison, and out of the criminal justice system entirely, continues. The work of the Pentonville project (see Chapter 5) is now undertaken as part of the normal workload of the welfare liaison unit in Pentonville. The studies of decision-making by the police and by magistrates each suggested specific areas for further investigation and these are being pursued. It is hoped that in the near future some new facilities will be made available in one or more localities to which the police may escort those found drunk and incapable rather than arresting them. These will be monitored to see what contribution they make to minimising contact between the persistent petty offender and the criminal justice system. Day centres emerged from discussions with magistrates and probation service representatives as promising resources to enable persistent petty offenders to be contained within the community, and further investigation is being undertaken accordingly. Continuing research, and various issues raised but not resolved by the empirical studies described in this volume, are discussed further in Chapter 7.

2 Social disadvantage among persistent petty offenders

Introduction

For a study of persistent offenders, Pentonville prison, regarded as the archetypal revolving door institution, had the advantage of having a large proportion of inmates who continually returned for minor depredations. Moreover it had the unique facility of the welfare liaison unit, which will be described later in this chapter and features in the experiment described in Chapter 5. It had been hoped to choose a prison for this exercise that received and discharged its population into a fairly small area. However, no such establishment could be discovered. Information supplied from prison index statistics showed that almost half of Pentonville's relevant population (men serving sentences of 12 months or less and fine defaulters) had been sentenced outside Greater London.

The study was confined to prisoners serving sentences of imprisonment and those committed in default of paying fines. Other sectors of the prison population, namely unsentenced prisoners awaiting trial or sentence of remand for reports; those awaiting deportation or subject to detention order; and civil prisoners, were excluded. This is not to say that similar problems are not experienced by the other types of prisoner; indeed, prison staff tended to view the civil prisoners, including some who remained in custody for lengthy periods, as the ones with the greatest social problems and fewest resources to cope with them, whether inside or outside prison. However, different remedies need to be sought in order to cope with the problems posed by other groups in the population.

Three separate samples were selected. The main one was of 50 men aged 30 and over, sentenced to imprisonment without the option of a fine. Two other groups were also studied to provide comparisons – 25 fine defaulters aged 30 and over, and 25 men aged under 30.

Sources of information

Information was gathered both from records and through interviews with individual offenders. The current prison file on each prisoner and any previous ones available were perused. The records kept by the welfare liaison unit, and any available from the probation officers, were searched for information about any welfare applications individuals had made. The letter sheets kept by the censor's office giving a complete record of all incoming and outgoing mail and all visiting orders sent out and taken up were inspected and a count made of all letters and visits, noting who the contacts were. Interviews were conducted

7

after the prison records had been seen so that the interviewers could be aware of which areas to probe. Although structured so that common ground was covered in each interview, these relied on open-ended questions covering the following topics: problems on release regarding accommodation and employment; contacts with the outside while in prison and social relationships when at liberty; and the use of the welfare liaison unit, the probation and after-care service and other facilities and attitudes towards these resources. Information was later collected from Criminal Record Office (CRO) records held at Scotland Yard. These provided additional information about social background as well as having fuller data on criminal history. CRO data were not collected for the sample of younger men.

The main sample
Selection
This sample, picked on 14 October 1977, was confined to men aged 30 and over serving sentences of up to 12 months. The prisoners to be included were selected at random from the nominal index box according to a stratified design, aimed at over-representing those convicted of the most trivial offences, and designed to give a final sample of 50 men. Every individual aged 30 or more serving up to and including 12 months was chosen. (As it happened no one serving more than nine months was selected, since allocation policies meant that there were very few in the population serving between nine and 12 months). Their records were inspected and those who had fewer than five previous convictions or whose records included offences of sex or violence, apart from the most trivial instances, were excluded. One man whose current offence was handling stolen goods was also excluded on the grounds that this might not have been a petty offence.

Basic characteristics
The age and sentence length distributions of the final sample are given below. Half of those selected were aged over 40. The men aged 50 and over were concentrated among those serving sentences of three months or less while those serving six months or more were younger on average than the rest.

Table 1
Age and length of sentence

	Length of sentence				
Age	up to and including 1 month	over 1 up to and including 3 months	over 3 up to and including 6 months	over 6 up to and including 9 months	Total
30–34	1	1	6	4	12
35–39	5	1	3	3	12
40–49	5		8	2	15
50–59	3	3	2		8
60+	1	2			3
Total	15	7	19	9	50

Theft, usually shoplifting, was by far the most numerous current offence, except among the very short sentences, where drunkenness and begging were both more prevalent. Because of the selection process, property offences were typically minor. Of the 25 for which details were recorded, nine involved attempts only and 12 included items of property each valued at less than £25.

Table 2

Type of current offence by length of sentence

Current main offence	up to and including 1 month	over 1 up to and including 3 months	over 3 up to and including 6 months	over 6 up to and including 9 months	Total
Violence (minor)	2		1	1	4
Enter as a trespasser/ Burglary	1	2	3		6
Theft/equipped	3	2	12	8	25
Handling		1			1
Deception		1	1		2
Taking and driving away			1		1
Criminal damage			1		1
Drunk and disorderly	5				5
Begging	4	1			5
Total	15	7	19	9	50

Criminal history

The sample had been confined to men having five or more previous convictions. Only seven men had fewer than 10 and half of those for whom information was available had 25 or more. In general those sentenced to the shortest sentences had the most previous convictions.

In general a substantial proportion of the previous sentences had been imprisonment. Only one man had no previous custody and a number had served sentences of preventive detention in the past. It must be noted that even when not sentenced to imprisonment many of these offenders spent time in custody – on remand or in default of payment of fines. A few of the sample when asked where they lived suggested that almost all their time was spent in prison.

Every prisoner on reception into Pentonville is asked the date of his last discharge from prison. Five of the sample had been out of prison less than a fortnight and a further 10 less than six weeks. On the other hand, nine had not been in prison for at least three years. Of those currently sentenced to one month or less only one had been at liberty for more than one year.

Table 3
Previous convictions by length of sentence[1]

Previous convictions	up to and including 1 month	over 1 up to and including 3 months	over 3 up to and including 6 months	over 6 up to and including 9 months	Total
5–9	2	1	2	2	7
10–14		2	3	3	8
15–19		1	3		4
20–24	1		5	1	7
25–29	1	1	3		5
30–39	4	1	1	1	7
40–49	1			1	2
50 or more	3	1	2		6
Total	12	7	19	8	46
Number unknown	3			1	4

Persistent petty offenders are often thought of as having life long experience of institutional care and penal institutions. Contrary to this, however, half the sample had not started to offend until they were adult (21 or older), a much larger proportion than in the general prison population and, even of those with juvenile records, only nine had ever been sentenced to borstal training. Among this group were individuals who had had a normal secure upbringing and had lived and worked and accepted responsibility with some personal disaster, such as being left by a wife or the death of a close family member. Many explanations of their present situations hinged on drinking behaviour, for example adopting excessive drinking habits in the army or merchant navy, which had led to an unsettled way of life. Drink appeared to be related to offending in the case of two thirds of the sample, either directly, through convictions for drunkenness, or indirectly in that, according to their own accounts, thieving and minor violence was attributed to the influence of alcohol.

Personal characteristics
To a great extent the findings about birthplace confirmed that the majority of the sample had drifted to London from far afield. This was particularly true of

[1] Even for those cases where information was culled from both prison and CRO records, the total number of previous convictions recorded was likely to be an under-estimate. This is because non-indictable offences are not required to be notified to CRO and only a minority of them are notified. Even some indictable ones are never forwarded to CRO. Police records kept by forces other than the Metropolitan police, available in the prison records of some men in the sample sentenced in courts outside London, only included those non-indictable offences reported to CRO or committed locally. Where two sets of information were available there were some wide discrepancies. An extreme example was a case of one prisoner whose CRO record showed 41 convictions while that in the prison file showed 81. Equally often the CRO record showed more than the prison file. Sometimes information from the prisoner himself, recorded on the (Standard Classification Form) would suggest fewer previous convictions than the record, sometimes more. For the current analysis the largest total was used.

those serving one month or less. (Two-thirds of them had been born in Scotland or Ireland and there was only one Londoner among them.) Only a quarter of the whole sample had been born in London. There were only three coloured men (all born in the West Indies) among them, a very low proportion compared to the general prison population.

Table 4
Place of birth by length of sentence

Birthplace	up to and including 1 month	over 1 up to and including 3 months	over 3 up to and including 6 months	over 6 up to and including 9 months	Total
London	1	2	8	2	13
Rest of England/Wales	4	2	4	1	11
Scotland	6	1	4	3	14
Ireland	4	1	2		7
Abroad		1	1	3	5
Total	15	7	19	9	50

There were three married men in the sample who were living with their wives at the time of sentence and a fourth who had been cohabiting for four years. Eighteen had, in the past, been married (six were separated, 11 divorced and one widowed) but the majority of the sample had always been single (28). Among the 46 without wives, only eight had, when arrested, any current relationships with a steady girlfriend or a cohabitee.

Nineteen men had some personal contact with people outside while in Pentonville, with those serving longer sentences being more likely to have had such contacts. All the four married men, but only two of the 28 single men, had received both visits and letters. Of the total of 31 men who had received neither, only seven were in touch with family or friends when at liberty. Another eight claimed they had casual acquaintances on the outside, leaving 16 who appeared to have absolutely no personal relationships however tenuous. However, it seemed that these men were not unable to make friends, as they appeared to relate reasonably well to those with whom they had to associate in prison.

Before interviewing the sample about accommodation problems some information was collected about the range of facilities for homeless men available at that time in central London. Anybody who is completely destitute could obtain a night's lodging at the Department of Health and Social Security reception centre at Consort Road, Peckham. This had room for 773 men in large dormitories. On admittance everyone had to undergo inspection for infestation and take a compulsory bath, and had to complete a 'task' before being discharged in the morning. Access to the four smaller reception centres with higher standard accommodation in the London area was normally through Consort Road. Emergency shelter, free for one night if necessary, was available at 'The Marmite' run by St Mungo Community Trust which housed 150 men in very rough premises. The Salvation Army ran a number of common lodging houses. Most of them offered accommodation in large dormitories, but two provided small dormitories, and Booth House in Whitechapel had single and double rooms and also ran a seven-day detoxification programme for up to ten men. The Church Army ran a hostel with accommodation in small dormitories and single cubicles catering for men who had employment and St Mungo's ran Old Charing Cross Hospital as a working men's hostel with 342 beds in dormitories. Other hostels were run as commercial ventures. Westminster City Council provided accommodation for 700 men in Bruce House, their common lodging house, and there were three Rowton House hotels in central London which provided accommodation in single and double cubicles. In outlying areas of London, and also in Brighton where five of the men in the sample had been arrested, there was accommodation available in bed and breakfast hotels. In these it was not uncommon for six, or even ten, men to share one room.

Accommodation

Accommodation was seen as a problem by the majority of the sample. Twenty had been living rough – either sleeping out all the time, or occasionally using Salvation Army hostels and cheap lodgings. Three had been in hostels run by the Salvation Army or the Church Army and another nine had been staying in commercial hostels or hotels. Only three men at arrest, had been living in settled accommodation, to which they could return on release. Forty men had not had a settled address in the recent past, thirty-one of them having had no fixed address for at least five years. Thirty-three men had slept rough on more than isolated occasions. Ten men habitually slept rough in the same areas of inner London but eighteen of the sample were mobile in terms of travelling around the country and altogether about two-thirds would be unlikely to stay in one place for very long. However this mobility is partly to seek better conditions of shelter, employment and free handouts, and some of it could probably be stemmed by offering alternatives based on a specific locality.

While some of the younger men in the sample claimed to have chosen to abandon a settled way of life, the older men tended to suggest that they had been forced by circumstances to sleep rough or resort to hostels. Lack of finances was blamed for their inability to make any improvement in their circumstances by those, the majority, who maintained they would now like to change their way of life. There was much antipathy to some of the facilities currently provided and some men claimed they slept rough in preference to using the available hostels. However, in discussion of their attitudes it emerged that they would generally welcome having a roof over their heads if certain conditions were different. They tended to object to the rules hostels imposed regarding hours of opening and alcohol, and a few complained about the dogma thrust at them by some of the establishments run by religious bodies. They objected to accommodation in large dormitories and were almost universally critical of the standards of hygiene in the large Salvation Army hostels. It was apparent from the interviews that provision would only be acceptable, and therefore used if it was reasonably clean and private and if the individual's drinking habits did not prohibit its retention. However, once these basic conditions were met their aspirations may not be too difficult to fulfil. ✗

Employment and social security
The great majority of the sample had been unemployed for a long time at arrest. Only six had been in regular employment immediately prior to this sentence and another four had had casual work. For most of the sample the employment problems mattered less to them than their other difficulties, but about a fifth of them would have welcomed help in this respect.

About three-quarters of those asked said that they claimed social security benefit and these men, including those sleeping rough who were given a special weekly allowance of £11.50 by the Supplementary Benefits Commission, seemed to find little or no difficulty in obtaining it. Those who did not claim were those in regular or casual employment and one man who lived by begging.

Drink
Excessive drinking appeared to be very widespread and ten men had had treatment for alcoholism. (On the other hand, there were only two drug addicts in the sample). Seventeen men appeared from interview and records evidence to have severe problems, associated with methyl alcohol, and another 18 appeared to have only slightly less serious problems of excessive alcohol consumption. Four men appeared to have sporadic drinking problems, in that drink led to offending or other types of trouble, for example losing accommodation. Only in seven cases was there no evidence of immoderate drinking. All but one of those serving the shortest sentences (one month or less) had serious drinking problems, and those whose convictions had started later in life tended to have worse drink problems than those with juvenile criminal records.

Use of facilities
The Welfare Liaison Unit and the Probation Department in Pentonville prison
At the time of this study the welfare liaison unit (WLU) was staffed by one principal prison officer, one senior prison officer, one basic grade prison officer and two probation officers. It undertook part of the work load normally dealt with in prisons by the probation department, in that it saw every prisoner serving less than three months on reception (whereas the separate probation department saw those serving longer terms) and all welfare applications went to it in the first instance. In general the WLU dealt with the most practical matters and passed on to probation department problems that needed intensive work by an individual probation officer. Only one of the sample had seen a probation officer during the present sentence, for help in sorting out his wife's social security benefit.

13

A large part of the workload of the WLU involved dealing with problems that demand contact with the outside world – obtaining payment of fines, informing relatives, recovering belongings – but, especially in the period just after its establishment (in 1972), it concentrated on accommodation and employment facilities for release. Given that this focus was still of central concern the use made of the WLU by the sample was surprisingly low. Altogether 15 of them had made an application by the time the records were inspected. Eight of these presented problems relating to communication with the outside (a recurring problem was recovering belongings left in railway stations, hostels etc.) Those men who applied for this type of help tended to be satisfied. Only one of the sample had requested help with employment but nothing had materialised by the time he was interviewed. Six men had completed the WLU form requesting help with accommodation but typically they expected to be dissatisfied with the results. However, one man had already received a positive response by the time he was interviewed. He had been seen by the social worker from the Catholic social services and been offered a place in a select hostel. He was diffident about accepting this but said he intended to do so in order not to disappoint the social worker. Of the large remainder who perceived themselves having accommodation problems the typical attitude to the WLU was that all it had to offer them were the most unacceptable hostels – the Salvation Army or Church Army ones in Central London, that it could not do anything for them that they could not do for themselves and that there was nothing that could be done for them from inside prison to alter their situation outside. They often based their attitudes on past experience long ago but were unwilling to give the facilities another try. By no means did all the sample understand what help they could ask for or were willing to use the facilities available.

The probation and after-care service outside the prison
Thirty-three of the sample had had some contact with the probation service outside the prison, mainly by virtue of sentences. Only seven had positive attitudes to it while 15 of them had negative ones and the remainder were indifferent. Another four, who had never actually used the probation and after-care service also had unfavourable attitudes. A distinction was drawn between 'the Borough' (the after-care office in the Borough High Street) and the probation and after-care service. The two were not considered as in any way related, as a number who were negatively disposed to the rest of the probation and after-care service were prepared to go for help to 'the Borough', which was seen as a source of free handouts. Even so, those who would approach the after care office were a small minority of the sample. The majority of the sample tended to feel that the probation and after-care service was irrelevant to them.

Treatment
Information about the use of other facilities that was collected in the interviews cannot be considered exhaustive. Although the subject was probed as closely as possible, it is likely that some interviewees omitted to report on some of the

resources they had used in the past. The records indicated some gaps, mainly where the individual had received mental hospital treatment as the result of a court order. The available information suggested a low incidence of mental hospital treatment for conditions other than alcoholism, compared to that recorded in other studies for example in the South East Prison Population Survey (cf Home Office Research Unit, Research Bulletin, No 5, 1978). Six had had spells in mental hospitals for general psychiatric treatment, in at least two cases for extensive stays, and one of the sample had been the subject of psychiatric diagnosis. Ten of the sample had received treatment for alcoholism, mainly hospital-based (St Bernard's, Southall, was repeatedly mentioned) and one of the sample had undergone aversion therapy in Grendon (which had cured him of gin, so that he now drank vodka!). Two of the sample in addition to using hospitals and alcoholic treatment units (which were mentioned only by a handful of men) had been to the Alcoholics Recovery Project, and had had periods in their dry house. One of the sample had arranged (he maintained by his own efforts, but some credit must go to the WLU) to go to a purpose-built alcoholics unit in Greenock on release. The two drug addicts in the sample had both received treatment.

Hostels and reception centres
The majority of the sample had some experience of the low end of the range of hostel provision but few had encountered the specialist end. One had been very comfortable in one of the Norman Houses, run by a charitable concern to accommodate ex-offenders, while another had rejected the very same facility. Another had been in a residential project run by NACRO and hoped to do so again on release from this sentence. The Rowton Houses, Bruce House (run by Westminster Council) and the Church Army hostels were generally thought of as being tolerable. Distinction was made between different hostels provided by the Salvation Army by some of the sample who had used its better provisions, but in general the shelter it afforded was seen as unacceptable and many preferred to sleep out rather than go to its dormitory-type hostels.

Not many of the sample had extensive experience of reception centres, but those who had made a distinction between the Camberwell reception centre at Gordon Road, which was seen as intolerable, and ones in other parts of the country. In general the reception centres were seen as interfering with freedom, but one of the sample had been content to go from Gordon Road to one of the day re-establishment centres and another said he would be prepared to go into a settlement wing.

Discharge grants
The majority of the sample were eligible for the 'homeless discharge grant' given to those thought to have nowhere to go on release. At the time of this study it amounted to £27.70 (as opposed to the ordinary grant of £12.80[2]).

---

[2] Discharge grant rates are reviewed annually and in November 1979 the respective sums were £39.95 and £16.35.

Those in the sample who hoped either to rent a room or to obtain bed and breakfast accommodation felt that the no fixed address grant was insufficient. Certainly, without additional resources it would not enable a man to obtain a bed-sit in London but it appeared to be sufficient for a week's board and lodging in either a commercial hostel or one run by the charitable organisations. For example, at that time it cost upwards of £7.20 a week for a single cubicle in a Rowton House, breakfast was about 45p a day and an evening meal about 75p. The Salvation Army offered bed and breakfast at £1.40 per day or £8.80 per week. However, the Rowton Houses were full every night and the Salvation Army, which had empty beds, tended to be rejected by the sample. For these reasons, the men maintained, it was impossible to obtain decent accommodation. There was a general suspicion among the prison staff that the money tended to be squandered and that the temptation to spend it on drink was so strong that the men did not contemplate saving sufficient for a week's board and lodging.✓

Overlap of problems

To investigate the overlap between the four major problem areas – accommodation, employment, drink (or drugs) and lack of social ties – each individual was rated as having a severe, moderate or negligible problem in each area.

Nineteen men in the sample had severe problems in every area. Moreover, their problems had already endured for a long time; for example, on average they had been of no fixed abode for 15 years. Eight had at some time been married but these marriages had typically ended long ago. They were indeed a group of persistent offenders despite the fact that 12 of them had only started to offend when adults. They all had more than 20 recorded offences, the average being about 40 and, given the under-recording of non-indictable offences, their total number of court appearances must be very large, such that this group does indeed disproportionately overburden the system. One down-and-out wine drinker, aged 57, in this group, had been a music hall artist. He preferred to stay in the Westminster City Council-run Bruce House but was sometimes forced to sleep rough. He was depressed, had a short memory such that he continually repeated himself and did not know where his cell was located, and was unkempt even in prison. Another wine drinker, aged 64, claimed he had Parkinson's disease and his leg shook continuously. He slept rough with others under the bridge at Charing Cross. Although cheerful about his way of life, he would like to have a place in a hostel. He considered he would still drink if he had a room but 'not to get drunk'. Two men in their late thirties both moved around fairly widely. One was from Belfast and had come to England for work. He had started drinking heavily as a teenager and now, despite being willing to work, rarely found either job or accommodation and survived through begging and shoplifting. The other, a divorced man from Lincolnshire, had drifted around the South, spending the majority of the past three years in Brighton where he had amassed 30 convictions for drunkenness. He had come into

Pentonville on this occasion with another down-and-out friend (also in the sample and in the same category) and they planned to try their luck in Portsmouth on release, feeling that the Brighton police knew them too well.

There were 13 men who each had three severe problems and were very similar to the previous group. Three of them had no drink problem. They comprised the only old age pensioner in the sample, a Pole and a West Indian aged only 30. The pensioner's major problem of accommodation, had found a possible solution during this sentence as he had been placed in a select hostel which might also provide a basis for improving his social ties. The Pole, whose physical condition appeared to be extremely poor, seemed to have fallen through the system of social provision. He claimed he had given up work through failing health but had received no benefit and had been living in the open in Hyde Park for 12 years surviving by begging. The young West Indian had been rejected by his parents, who lived in London, and slept rough around Piccadilly Circus where he was frequently arrested by the police for being a suspected person.

Five men each had two severe problems, drink or drugs invariably one of them. The two whose additional severe problem was accommodation (having been of no fixed abode for five and 15 years respectively) were particularly badly placed. Another five men had a severe drink problem but only moderate or negligible problems in every other area. They seemed to realise their need to change their drinking habits and three of them had had treatment for alcoholism. In one case a stay in an alcoholics recovery project house had led to a few months of being dry before the relapse which led to the current offence.

The remaining eight men in the sample were relatively well placed, having no severe problems apart from long-term unemployment. They were not as persistent in their offending as the other groups, having between five and 14 previous convictions, and eight on average. One of them appeared to have no problems at all and his criminal history was atypical in that it was five years since his last conviction.

Identifying a core group
The 32 men with severe problems in all or three of the four areas constituted an extreme group. They had an average of twice as many (32 compared to 16) previous convictions as the men with fewer severe problems and also differed in other basic characteristics. They were older than the rest of the sample; all those over 50 years fell in this extreme group with multiple problems. The average age of those with problems in all four areas was 48 years compared to 44 years for those with three severe problems and 36 years for the rest. Those with most problems were serving shorter sentences. All but one of the men sentenced to one month or less had severe difficulties in three or four areas and only two of those serving more than six months fell in this core group.

Current offence was related to severity of problems in that all ten of those convicted of drunk and disorderly or begging fell in the core group – all but two of them having severe problems in all four areas. Over half of this group had committed property offences, but these were typically trivial. The following examples illustrate the cases that came within the core group:

'A' was sentenced to six months for attempted burglary. He had 60 convictions over a 30 year period and since 1960 exactly half of these were for obtaining pecuniary advantage by deception, through ordering and consuming meals in restaurants and being unable to pay for them.

'B' had a long history of mental institutionalisation and had been in hospital as recently as 1976. He slept rough when not in hospital. He was serving three months for theft of milk and clothes. Seven of his 24 previous convictions were simply theft of milk.

'C' was clearly an alcoholic. He behaved in a bizarre way when in prison and was rarely at liberty for more than a matter of days. He was released from Pentonville on 28 September 1977, was sentenced to one month for being drunk and disorderly the following day, was released again on 29 October, and sentenced to three months for criminal damage the very next day.

'D' had three days out of Pentonville before his current sentence of 28 days for begging. He had lived rough for 20 years, mainly in the Leicester Square area of London, where he was frequently arrested for being drunk and disorderly.

The comparison samples
When selecting the samples for comparison only partial information about criminal histories was available. The two samples were later analysed therefore to see what proportion came within the definition of persistent petty offender (in terms of having five or more previous convictions and no serious offences of violence or sex in their records) and to see what proportion resembled the core group which accounted for two-thirds of the main sample.

Among the 25 male fine defaulters aged 30 or over who were interviewed, seven were later found not to fit the criterion of having five or more previous convictions and were excluded from further analysis. The rest fell into two distinct groups. One group of ten men was not at any great disadvantage. Seven of them had relatively settled accommodation, six usually had some sort of employment and only two admitted dependence on drink or drugs. Their average age was 40 years and on average they had 12 recorded convictions. Seven of them were in prison for theft. The other group was composed of eight men (ie almost half those eligible for consideration) who had on average at least 26 convictions. They suffered extreme disadvantage and all of them were vagrant and drank heavily. Their average age was 45. Five of them were in prison as a result of a drunkenness offence, two for begging and one for criminal damage. The following two case histories demonstrate the similarity of these men to the core group among those sentenced to imprisonment.

'E', serving seven days, had been fined £10 for a drunkenness offence and failure to surrender to bail. He had 30 previous convictions, 15 of which had resulted in prison sentences. Born in Dublin he was 39 and was blind in one eye as a result of an accident in which he fractured his skull. He blamed his drink problem (he mixed cider and mandrax) on this accident. His wife left him in 1960 and he has lived rough for 10 years.

'F', serving 14 days, had been fined £5 for two offences of begging. His 26 previous convictions had mainly led to fines and he had been sentenced to imprisonment only three times. He drunk wine, cider and meths and had been in trouble since he started drinking at age 19, being now 44 years. He spent whatever money he obtained on gambling. He last worked and had 'decent accommodation' in 1973.

Among the group of 25 prisoners aged under 30, four were fine defaulters and the rest had been sentenced to imprisonment. Eleven men did not fit the criterion of having five or more previous convictions but, given that many of the core group of older men were late starters in terms of criminal career, the information collected on all 25 men was scrutinised to identify those who might be expected to become like the core group. Eight men seemed well settled with accommodation, employment and social ties and appeared very unlikely to degenerate to any great extent. Two of them were fine defaulters and four of them first offenders. Twelve were possible candidates (one of them a fine defaulter) and they had an average of nine previous convictions. They currently had social contacts and places to live but if these, often tenuous, arrangements broke down they could drift into the core group pattern. Five men, a fifth of the sample, seemed even more likely to be future core group members. They had between six and 12 convictions and included one fine defaulter. They were already unsettled with regards to accommodation and employment. Three were single, one had a broken marriage and the other's marriage was at breaking point. Drugs were mentioned in three cases. The following case illustrates the similarity with their older counterparts:

'G' was a Glaswegian aged 28 and had ten previous convictions. He was serving a three month sentence for shoplifting a jacket from a large store. He had had no fixed address at arrest and his plans for obtaining a job and somewhere to live on release were extremely unrealistic. He said his brothers and sisters had rejected him, and there was no one to offer him friendship or practical help. His record described him as a 'loner' and noted an 'obvious drink problem'.

Although there were already strong indications that these men would end up like the older sample, their relative youth gave at least some hope that intervention to alter their circumstances might lead to a change in their patterns of behaviour and they might desist from offending. The provision of facilities to meet their needs might possibly aid individuals' reform and thus effect future saving to the criminal system.

The size of the problem

The drawback of doing an exercise in a single prison is the difficulty that it presents in generalising to the whole of the country. The results of this exercise suggest that at any one time there would be about 150 older petty persistent offenders as defined for this exercise, among the sentenced population in Pentonville, and about 600 such men would be coming into Pentonville during a year. Of these, 100 in the population at a given time and 500 among those received in any year would suffer severe multiple disadvantage, like the core group identified in this exercise. However, some individuals will be counted repeatedly in the reception figures since they return again and again to prison during the course of a year.

By virtue of serving short sentences, persistent petty offenders tend to be concentrated in local prisons rather than to be evenly distributed. Prison statistics suggest that Pentonville has substantially more men serving sentences of 12 months or less who have five or more previous convictions than any other establishment, but Liverpool and Manchester each have over a hundred such men. Using the findings of this study, it was estimated that there were about 1,700 cases fitting those criteria in the prisons in England and Wales on 30 June 1977 and about 900 of them were probably like the core group. These figures have important limitations in that the criteria used for defining persistent petty offenders are arbitrary and choosing different ones would of course alter the size of the group. Moreover, they have been selected among only a small part of the prison population, namely men aged 30 or more sentenced to imprisonment. There would, of course, be offenders with similar records and characteristics among the fine defaulters and also among the younger population.

Stereotyping the persistent petty offender

There is a general tendency to devise labels to categorise problem groups and this study provided an opportunity to see how far various labels generally applied to this group are appropriate. One such label is 'socially inadequate'. Despite the use of 'socially' in the label, it tends to suggest personal shortcomings and to attribute blame to individuals for their failures. On inspection these overtones seemed unwarranted. While there was no method by which this study could assess their personal ability to cope, those interviewed tended to suffer from severe social problems that would make life difficult for the most adequate of persons.

'Vagrant' is a label that cannot be applied to the whole group. Although the majority of the sample originally came to London from elsewhere most of them were not wanderers continuing to drift around the country but stayed more or less in the same area. However, in that many of them lacked conventional community ties and had no settled accommodation they tended to fit the 'homeless and rootless' or 'down and out' stereotype.

Even though many of the sample had a history of drunkenness offending and, in an even larger number of cases, their drink problems and their offending were apparently associated, the label 'habitual drunken offender' is also an oversimplification. Again this label does not apply to the whole group; more-over, it concentrates on a feature that is difficult to alter, in that many problem drinkers are unwilling to change their drinking behaviour or even to acknow-ledge it as a problem, and that may constitute as much a reaction to circum-stances as personal choice. This study indicated an association between multiple disadvantage and persistent petty offending. As extremity in terms of dis-advantage increased, persistent of offending (or rather, frequency of conviction) also tended to increase. Some of the welfare problems would need to be tackled if any change in personal situations were to be achieved. In terms of purely criminal policy, however, persistent petty offender remains the most appropriate designation in that it focusses on problems amenable to criminal justice decision making: the triviality of offending and its frequency of repetition, matters readily identifiable at most stages of the process, and in relation to which different decisions are possible.

Planning intervention

Catering more adequately for the group's social disadvantage appears to be a necessary prerequisite for keeping them out of the criminal justice system. However there seems limited scope for achieving this. Lack of supportive contacts and isolation from the settled community appear to be very relevant, but these are not problems that can be easily solved. Neither is the problem of excessive drinking among men who are not prepared to change. From the study, it seemed possible that some excessive drinking is due to loneliness, boredom or having nowhere to call home nor even a place to sleep, in which case the pro-vision of more adequate resources, particularly accommodation, might indirectly alleviate alcohol problems. Chronic unemployment was a widespread charac-teristic, but this problem was perceived as incidental by virtue of being over-shadowed by more pressing needs. However, there was a universal need for some occupation to fill empty hours and to provide companionship other than by drinking. The widespread accommodation problem appears to be the most worthwhile to tackle first because of its apparent primacy to the interviewees themselves and the way in which it can be considered fundamental to the other problem areas.

However, the provision of additional facilities by itself is unlikely to bring about the desired reduction in the burden on the criminal justice system. In the case of the older men with which the study was mainly concerned it would be over-ambitious to expect that even a massive improvement in their circum-stances would lead to any appreciable change in their criminal behaviour. Intervention therefore would have to be directed towards changing the system to make alternative responses to the same behaviour. There appeared to be three points at which there might be scope for making different decisions in

21

order to minimise contact between the persistent petty offender and the criminal justice system. The first was the point of arrest. More of the group's nuisance behaviour could possibly be tolerated or ignored or otherwise reacted to without the police making an arrest and subsequently preferring a charge. The second was the point of sentence. Magistrates could perhaps impose fewer custodial sentences on persistent petty offenders and avoid sentences that led indirectly to prison, particularly fines levied on individuals lacking the means to pay, and make instead greater use of facilities that might help them to settle in the community. The third was the point of release from prison. More effort might be made to resettle these persistent petty offenders who did get sent to prison in the hope of at least increasing the period before subsequent reconviction and return to prison. Separate studies were planned to investigate the possibilities for intervention at each of these decision making points, and these are the subject of Chapters 3 to 5.

3 Police interaction with homeless petty offenders

Introduction

Arrest by the police constitutes the initial entry point to the criminal justice system. Diversion at this decision point, therefore, effects more savings of time, effort and resources for the criminal justice system than at any subsequent point. In order to discover the way in which the police already exercise discretion, and to see if there was scope for further diversion, two short studies focussed on the way in which the police come into contact with homeless petty offenders.

The first study, undertaken between October 1978 and January 1979, covered three areas in the Metropolitan Police District (MPD). The second, during August to October 1979 was a replication to discover if there were common problems and similar methods of coping with them elsewhere. Brighton was selected, because it appeared to have a high concentration of the relevant types of people, and ten per cent of the sample of persistent petty offenders in the Pentonville descriptive study (described in Chapter 2) had been arrested there.

Methods of study

The study was intended principally to be observation of day-to-day police procedure. The researcher spent most of the fieldwork periods accompanying the police, mainly mobile patrols (but also beat police officers in the Central London area). This was mostly carried out in the late afternoon, the evening and the early hours of the morning since these periods appeared to be the busiest for the type of incident in which the researcher was interested. Discussion with police officers of various ranks from constable to superintendent was mainly informal, in the course of spending time in and around the police stations. In order to put the researcher's observations into its wider context an analysis was made of all charges during one month of the study periods (November 1978 in the MPD, July 1979 in Brighton). In Brighton, due to the infrequency of relevant events being actually observed, qualitative data were collected from a variety of records: files prepared for prosecution of a number of relevant charges at the magistrates' court, 'refused charges' ie sheets prepared on persons who were brought to the police station but not subsequently charged, and the records kept by the collator on individual offenders who were identified as members of the relevant group.

In Brighton, cases observed at the arrest stage were followed through the magistrates courts wherever possible. Consequently a substantial proportion of the researcher's time was spent in court and other relevant material was gathered there. Additional data were collected from the courts serving two of the MPD police stations. Bow Street magistrates' court (where a number of defendants convicted for drunkenness offences were interviewed) and West London magistrates' court. The researcher also contacted various agencies engaged in providing facilities for the homeless and for alcoholics to discuss their perception of the problem and their contact with the police. In Hammersmith, the researcher also interviewed park keepers and lavatory attendants who, in the course of their everyday duties, may have a lot of dealings with the vagrant population.

The areas studied
The period of observation in the MPD was mid-October 1978 to mid-January 1979. Its timing is important in that there is less vagrancy and less public drunkenness during the winter months than during the summer. Indeed, when the weather suddenly became very cold at the end of November there was a marked drop in activity of any kind. A list of areas of the MPD which were thought likely to have a sizeable number of homeless petty offenders was drawn up and from this the three police stations that volunteered for the study were:

i Bow Street
The area covered by this station includes Leicester Square, Covent Garden, the Strand and a stretch of the Embankment. Tourists are a major concern. Both traders' associations and the Westminster City Council are concerned with the effects on the attractiveness of the district of the presence of numerous vagrants. There are two large common lodging houses in the area, Bruce House run by the local authority, and the Old Charing Cross Hospital run by St Mungo's Community Trust, and a third, Arlington House, nearby. Covent Garden market used to provide employment for a significant number of casual workers and there is still a demand for such labour in the hotels and restaurants. Soup runs organised by the Salvation Army and St Mungo's normally cater for between 70 and 100 persons sleeping in the streets, and even more in the summer.

ii Bethnal Green
Until fairly recently the area included much derelict property. There are still expanses of waste ground where there were gipsy encampments at the time of the study. There is a complex of facilities for homeless persons run by the Salvation Army within the area and Spitalfields Church crypt provides shelter for men trying to escape from skid row. There are other common lodging houses in the immediate vicinity. Spitalfields market (just outside the boundary) and Whitechapel market employ casual labour. Local residents appear to be fairly tolerant of the behaviour of the vagrants in their district.

iii Hammersmith
During the 1960s major roadworks and building development led to an influx of labourers, predominantly single Irishmen. There used to be a Rowton House hotel catering for this group, but now they are accommodated in overcrowded bed and breakfast hotels, with 10 or more men sleeping in one

room in extreme cases. There is a small group of men who live in derelict buildings and who congregate on Hammersmith Broadway, in Furnival Gardens or Ravenscourt Park during the day. Analysis of data on homeless offenders in the area revealed that Irishmen were much more frequently represented there than in the other two districts, comprising 51 per cent of such offenders in Hammersmith, 35 per cent in Bethnal Green and 16 per cent in Bow Street.

The Brighton study was mainly done in the late summer, a period after the peak frequencies of public drunkenness and vagrancy offending. The analysis of charges covered the two sub-divisions in Brighton but the majority of the observational periods were in the sub-division which covered the west part of the town including the town centre and the popular part of the sea-front, since this was the busy area in respect of relevant incidents. There is a reception centre in the town and cheap bed and breakfast hotels which accepts vouchers from the Department of Health and Social Security (DHSS). There were a few squats used by the homeless who also slept out in shelters, under upturned boats on the beach or under bushes in parks.

Definition of the group
At the point of arrest the police frequently do not have details of criminal careers so the definition of persistent petty offender used in the initial study in Pentonville was inappropriate. A simple operational definition of the persons of relevance to the study was needed which could be applied rapidly and universally while in the field. As the descriptive study had shown that virtually all the core group of petty persistent offenders were homeless, this was taken as the defining characteristic. Only those homeless persons aged 21 or over were considered. 'Homelessness' was held to mean having no permanent address, and included those recorded as of 'no fixed abode' (NFA) and others living in lodging houses or similar establishments.

In Bow Street and Bethnal Green there was only a small number of large common lodging houses and these were easily picked up from the charge sheet. The situation was, however, more complicated in Hammersmith. There the homeless group used two distinct types of accommodation. The police divided them into 'skippers' (squatting in a derelict building) and 'kippers' (having a bed in a multi-occupied room in a so called 'bed and breakfast hotel' or 'guest house'). The police were aware of the addresses of the most notorious of the latter and the researcher identified others, but it is likely that some men living in 'kipper' conditions have been recorded as having a settled address. Thus the assessment of the proportion of homeless among the Hammersmith offenders may be misleadingly low. In Brighton the police knew the addresses of establishments that were used by the homeless and had the reputation of being 'doss houses'. According to the police the notorious ones were grossly overcrowded and they were aware of occasional flagrant abuses of the DHSS voucher system, which were extremely difficult to prove.

Analysis of charges

In the MPD stations studied, charge sheets were separated into 'major' and 'minor' crimes, roughly equivalent to indictable and non-indictable offences. No such convenient distinction was made in Brighton, so that it was necessary to categorize offences for analysis. The analysis included only charges against those aged 21 or over. Only a negligible proportion of charges against the homeless group appeared to be the result of executed warrants and these were excluded for the purposes of this analysis. A striking difference between the two studies is that drunkenness charges were much more common in the MPD (46 per cent of all charges recorded), than in Brighton (21 per cent).

Types of offending

Table 5 shows, by police station, for various types of offence, the percentage who were homeless.

Table 5

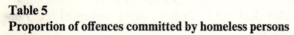

Proportion of offences committed by homeless persons

Offence type	Police station				
	Bow St	Bethnal Green	Hammersmith	All MPD areas	Brighton
Indictable	18%	7%	15%	15%	14%
Non-indictable	59%	60%	40%	52%	39%
Drunk	78%	74%	43%	64%	52%
Drunk and disorderly	52%	29%	46%	44%	44%
Begging	(100%)	(100%)	(100%)	(100%)	(100%)
Other minor offences	24%	15%	23%	22%	20%
Total	40%	43%	29%	37%	23%

(Figures in brackets are based on totals of offences less than 10)

It can readily be seen that homeless offenders were much over-represented among the minor offences, compared to the major ones, and within the minor offences were predominantly charged with begging, simple drunkenness, and, to a lesser extent, being drunk and disorderly. There are differences between the three areas of the MPD with Bow Street being closest to the overall pattern, Bethnal Green exhibiting the same trends to a more extreme extent, and Hammersmith having a lower proportion of homeless offenders altogether, and especially so for simple drunkenness. Homeless persons were responsible for a smaller proportion of offences in Brighton than in the MPD, a result almost entirely due to their figuring less prominently among arrests for drunkenness offences. The Brighton results, however, closely resemble those obtained in Hammersmith.

The actual numbers of offences committed by homeless persons are shown in Table 6.

Table 6

Numbers of offences committed by homeless persons

Offence types	Police station				
	Bow St	Bethnal Green	Hammersmith	All MPD areas	Brighton
Indictable	21	4	18	43	27
Non-indictable	79	75	61	215	38
Drunk	53	67	39	159	22
Drunk and disorderly	10	4	13	27	8
Begging	6	1	2	9	2
Other minor offences	10	3	7	20	8
Total	100	79	79	258	65

From these figures it can be seen that most homeless offenders are charged with minor offences, very largely simple drunkenness. Again Bow Street follows the general MPD pattern and Bethnal Green more extremely so. Hammersmith differs only in its relatively high percentage of offenders charged with drunk and disorderly. The pattern of arrests of homeless persons in Brighton was clearly different from that observed in the MPD. In Brighton their arrests were far more likely to be for indictable offences and far less likely to be for drunkenness. Very few of the homeless persons charged were female. There were only nine women among the 258 charged in the MPD and three women among the 65 charged in Brighton.

Police contact with homeless offenders

The extent to which the police appeared to have discretion about arresting homeless persons depended greatly on the type of offence involved.

Indictable offences

As far as indictable offences were concerned, the police stated that they had very little opportunity for exercising discretion if a case came to their notice. This was especially the case with property offences, which in fact accounted for most of the charges indictable against homeless persons. In the MPD it was the usual practice that the victim of property offences would be the person making the charge. Charges under the Theft Act, 1968 could also arise in two other circumstances in the MPD, when the police witnessed the actual theft or when they discovered stolen property on stopping and searching a person (under their powers in Section 66 of the Metropolitan Police Act, 1839). These situations could give individual police officers some discretion. One woman police constable at Bow Street felt that every such case had to be prosecuted: 'If the police spot even a petty theft, for example one bread roll from a delivery to a shop, they have to arrest them'. Another at the same station said she would go out of her way to avoid arrest in these circumstances. If, for instance, she saw a person steal a bottle of milk from a doorstep she would 'stop' the person (ie ask his name and address and check whether he was wanted in connection with any offence or warrant); if there was no record of previous convictions she would attempt to persuade him to return the milk and, if successful, not make an arrest. Deterrence is also a consideration in the decision to arrest for petty thefts. To quote a senior official, "In a place such as Brighton a fairly firm line must be adopted in exercising police discretion over theft from shops, especially by homeless persons, otherwise if too lenient an approach were adopted the problem would escalate and get out of hand".

Six of the 27 homeless persons charged with indictable offences in Brighton, received sentences of imprisonment (four of them having been convicted of shoplifting food or drink) another two were sent immediately to prison for fine default and eight, some of them eventually dealt with by non-custodial sentences, were remanded in custody. Information about disposal was not as readily available from the MPD stations studied but the impression gained was that a lower proportion of offenders experienced custodial sentences or were remanded in custody.

Non-indictable offences
Begging
Begging is an offence where the police both in the MPD and Brighton appeared to exercise discretion. Complaints from the public were rare, even in Bow Street and Brighton where visitors might have been expected to experience it as a nuisance. In Bethnal Green, the researcher was informed, there was "a lot of begging going on" but the police did not see it happen very often and took action "even less often". Usually the police would give a warning before they made an arrest. As one police constable in Bow Street said "if I see a bloke begging I tell him to clear off, if he returned the same day I arrest him". Observation suggested that the presence of a policeman was sufficient to make beggars move away.

In the MPD, in general only cases where requesting money was accompanied by threats of abuse would the police make an arrest. A distinction was made between persons playing musical instruments and those not. Buskers were seen as providing a service and would, therefore, never be arrested on a charge of begging although, if causing a nuisance, they might be arrested for obstruction. On one occasion when the researcher witnessed a woman police officer's interchange with a man who had been begging on the steps of the entrance to Charing Cross Station, the police officer asked the man to play his mouth organ for her in order to establish whether he played well enough to be rendering a service. The police officer's judgement was that the man was able to play the mouth organ and arrest was, therefore, not warranted. The man (who was somewhat inebriated) behaved, meanwhile, in a surly fashion and more or less demanded to be arrested. The police officer proceeded to make a CRO check with the Criminal Records Office over her personal radio. That completed she told the man to go on his way and keep out of her sight.

In Brighton the use of charges of begging had declined. Five years ago patrols kept watch for those 'mumping' (to use the local expression) and arrested those seen. Now, although the police were aware that the offending continued, they were not particularly concerned with it. A few of the regular homeless offenders were considered to be responsible for most of the begging. Of one of the most well known 'mumpers', often to be found playing the spoons or the mouth organ in the shopping precincts frequented by tourists, a police constable said "we only deal with him when there are complaints from shopkeepers and then we usually advise him to try his luck elsewhere". It was suggested that some magistrates would not accept that playing a musical instrument constituted begging but one of the two offenders charged in July had been playing a guitar and singing to a large group of persons. He refused to move when instructed and was arrested, he was conditionally discharged by the court.

One charge notable for its complete absence from either study was that of wandering abroad. Police constables in all three MPD stations were aware that they were discouraged from making such charges, although one policeman at Hammersmith said that he had used it on one occasion. At Bow Street it was the policy not to employ it, feeling that there was no 'accessible place where shelter was provided free of charge' to which vagrants could be directed since the reception centre at Peckham was considered too distant. In the past a record had been kept in Brighton of warnings given to those who persistently slept out and offenders in those days were charged with wandering abroad. This practice had lapsed and no officer interviewed there could recall any recent use of this charge.

Drunkenness offences

The researcher gained the impression from interviews and observation that the police exercised other discretion to minimise the number of arrests they made for drunkenness and were especially loth to arrest 'vagrants' for these offences. Despite that fact, forty-four per cent of all the charges made in November at the three stations studied in the MPD were for offences of drunkenness and 60 per cent of those charged were homeless offenders. Police in the MPD tended to see drunks as a nuisance they could well do without. Drunks as far as the police interviewed were concerned were a drain on resources which could be utilised more productively. They occupied space in police cells, often soiling them, they tended to take up more police time than other offenders – for example drunks in the cells are supposed to be checked at half-hourly intervals (as opposed to hourly) and often demand almost constant attention; and they frequently required medical attention, which incurred additional cost. However, given that a large proportion of police officers patrolling the streets in central London are probationers, drunks appeared to have one useful role as far as the

P Metropolitan police were concerned. Inspectors in charge of reliefs (shifts) felt that they should encourage probationers to make drunkenness arrests for the sake of experience in handling and searching offenders and the procedure of making a charge. Probationers, in their turn were aware that their 'figures' (the number of their arrests, 'stops' and 'processes', ie checks on motor vehicles) were being monitored and felt it important to "be seen in the charge room by supervising officers". Although officers with some years service maintained that there was much less pressure on today's recruit than when they were themselves probationers, the current probationers still felt they had to make regular arrests.

Q Two reasons were advanced for arresting drunks. The first is a matter of social control: a person is arrested for drunkenness in the public interest if he or she is fighting, being abusive, urinating in the street or otherwise causing affront. The second is a matter of providing a service: a person is arrested for drunkenness for his or her own protection if he or she is likely to come to harm if left to his or her own devices. In many cases, of course, both reasons may be applicable. Intervention by the public is relatively rare and is more often directed at securing help for the offender than a complaint about nuisance behaviour. However, when a member of the public calls for an ambulance to attend to someone, if the ambulance crew recognise that the person is simply drunk and incapable, they may radio for the police to make an arrest rather than take the individual to hospital, so that an attempt to help is converted into a criminal charge.

In the course of observation in the MPD station the researcher was present during 18 arrests for drunkenness. Ten of these were for the person's own protection, including two cases where an ambulance had been called. These cases provided a wide range of incidents. Only one was during daylight hours – an old man slumped on a seat in Leicester Square and foaming at the mouth. One man arrested at Bethnal Green was in need of medical attention – his ear had been half-severed from his head and the police felt that a hospital would be unwilling to deal with him in his drunken state. At the police station the divisional surgeon was called and stitched him up within half an hour. He thus speedily received the medical care he needed which otherwise he might have found difficult to obtain. Of the two cases that were handed over to police by ambulance crews one had been rolling about on the pavement, refusing to get up and claiming to be injured, and the other was in a very depressed state of mind and pleaded not to be charged.

The researcher was informed that only extreme behaviour led to charges of disorderly behaviour while drunk. This was borne out by observation, in that only two of the incidents witnessed in the MPD resulted in such charges, even though the majority of the individuals arrested created a good deal of disturbance at some time during the process of being taken to the police station and being charged. At Hammersmith the police considered a high proportion of those charged with drunkenness could also be charged with assault on police

30

officers. Such a combination was in fact infrequent, there being only two among the November 1978 charges at Hammersmith and none in the other two stations in that month. The higher incidents of drunk and disorderly charges at Hammersmith may reflect the greater concentration of vagrant Irish ex-labourers there. However, the police in that area appeared also to be less conciliatory there than at Bethnal Green, which had the lowest proportion of such charges. This may reflect the fact that the population of drunken offenders in Hammersmith includes many more people of settled address, whose behaviour was generally more disruptive than the average vagrant's. The police are then likely to anticipate trouble and to act more severely.

The incidence of arrests of members of the homeless group for drunkenness in Brighton was low relative to that in the areas of the MPD studied. As in the MPD, an arrest for being drunk and incapable was usually for a person's protection for example, when an individual was incapable of walking without falling over or had collapsed on the pavement. In such instances it was not unusual for an ambulance to have been summoned by a member of the police first. Another circumstance in which arrests were made was when persons were discovered asleep in the open, for example in shelters along the sea-front. One homeless individual arrested in such a place at 12.30 at night was very indignant when he appeared in court. Although he pleaded guilty, he stated, "I think it's ridiculous that I was done for drunk when I was lying asleep harming nobody". Charges of being drunk and disorderly were not infrequently the result of individuals being observed urinating in public or smashing bottles. However, being verbally abusive, either to members of the public, or to the police when there were others present, was sufficient to constitute disorder. Fairly frequently charges of assault on the police were preferred in conjunction with drunkenness charges. It was acknowledged that police officers who were completing their probationary period were more likely than their more experienced colleagues to arrest homeless drunks and on the occasions when there was a drunk to be dealt with more senior constables would, if convenient, attempt to take a newer recruit to the scene to make the arrest.

Drunks in public places tended to be moved on. The researcher observed the following incident in the mid-afternoon on a Thursday during August. There had been two complaints earlier in the day of a group of drunks and the third complaint was received while the patrol car crew, the inspector and another constable were present together. Two cars therefore went to the scene. Three men and one woman were sitting on the grass in the Pavilion grounds behind members of the public who were listening to the band. There were empty cider bottles beside them. When asked to leave, one of the men, all of whom were visibly drunk, called one of the constables "an animal". Another of the men tried to calm the situation saying "Come on, they are giving us a chance, don't be rude". The group removed the rubbish from the grass and left as instructed. Other attempts at moving drunks failed, however, and charges resulted as the following two incidents, details of which were abstracted from statements made by the arresting officers, illustrate:

> . . . as a result of information from a member of the public [the constable found the offender] attempting to touch a baby in a pram . . . [The constable] said to him "go away and let this lady pass". (The offender) took a few paces and fell to the ground!

The offender was arrested for being drunk and incapable:

> During the early afternoon a man was found asleep on a bench in the Pavilion Grounds. The constable woke him and told him to get on his way. The man became verbally abusive. The constable warned him not to use such language but the man persisted. The constable proceeded to arrest him for being drunk and disorderly. The man then "lashed out with both of his fists" and when the police vehicle arrived became so violent that it necessitated the assistance of other officers to get him inside it.

In general the officers interviewed felt that when a person refused to move on as instructed in the presence of members of the public, the police had no alternative but to make an arrest.

In Brighton not all arrests for drunkenness led to charges being preferred. Officers could recall occasions when there had been insufficient evidence to charge and there were two such instances among the 'refused charges' during July. There was also one case of an offender being cautioned after originally being arrested as drunk and incapable. A resident of a common lodging-house in London was in Brighton on a day trip organised by St Mungo's and had wandered off from the rest of the group and got drunk. After being cautioned he was released to the care of staff from St Mungo's.

Once charged, homeless drunkenness offenders faced more severe penalties in Brighton than in the MPD. In the MPD courts observed, the majority of homeless drunks were sentenced to a small fine (on average £3 for being drunk and incapable) or one day's imprisonment. This in effect was simply a nominal punishment, since their appearance in court counted as the day's imprisonment and they were not required to pay the fine. In Brighton, however, fines ranged from £5 to £25. Moreover, six of these fined were given no time to pay and, failing to do so, were dispatched immediately to Pentonville. Alternatives, of seven or fourteen days imprisonment, were set at initial appearance in three other Brighton cases where there was no likelihood of payment being made, and many of the others would be likely to be brought back to court and be imprisoned eventually for non-payment. In only one case was one day's imprisonment used as an alternative to a fine.

One offender arrested in Brighton for drunkenness was remanded in custody for three weeks for reports. The circumstances of the case are highly typical but illustrate well the confusion of social control and concern about protection

32

of the individual which may account for homeless persons being imprisoned for very trivial offences. The offender was a man in his middle fifties sharing a room in one of the bed and breakfast establishments used by the homeless. An ambulance crew requested police assistance in tracing a man who had been repeatedly telephoning from a public kiosk requesting an ambulance. The constable found him and told him to stop abusing the 999 system. The man refused saying he would keep ringing and that he wanted to be taken to a mental hospital (where he had been an in-patient some years ago). He was arrested for being drunk and incapable. He appeared in court the following day, a Saturday, which meant there was no probation officer readily available. In discussion with the court clerk the magistrates said "we cannot let him go in this state" and the defendant was told "we are keeping you inside for your own safety". Bail was refused on the grounds of the individual's safety.

Other interaction with homeless persons
Under Section 44 of the Vagrancy Act, 1824, and, in the MPD, Section 66 of the Metropolitan Police Act, 1839 the police have powers to stop persons in the street, question them and under the latter statute, search them. The police from Bow Street did 'stops' with much greater frequency than those in the other two areas in the MPD probably because their area attracts large numbers of strangers passing through. In Brighton also, the police used this procedure, known there as a 'check' to establish an individual's identity and discover, by radioing to the Police National Computer Unit, whether there were outstanding warrants for him or her. The procedure sometimes led to an arrest. For example, men were discovered sleeping in the doorway of a shop in the Strand at 1.20 a.m. All were questioned under Section 4 of the Vagrancy Act, 1824 and CRO checks made. There was an outstanding warrant (for non-appearance at court) for one of them and he was arrested.

Altogether it was the researcher's experience, which was confirmed in discussion, that the majority of police encounters with homeless persons did not result in arrest. In general the police in the MPD study were at great pains to avoid arresting those they identified as 'vagrants'. This reluctance of course only extended to minor infringements of the law, such as wandering abroad and drunkenness, and not to more serious crime, such as an assault or theft. Their reasons for the desire to minimise their involvement with this group are easy to appreciate. They did not want to experience the smell nor run the risk of infection. Searching them could be very unpleasant. Vagrants who were arrested in a louse-ridden state had to be disinfected. For this purpose they had to be driven to a cleansing station or reception centre. The van used would then be out of operation while it was cleansed, and the police constables who had handled the vagrant would have to be disinfested themselves. Sergeants were concerned about offensive smells and infestation being brought into the charge room and the cells. One sergeant maintained that he refused to tolerate the arrest of vagrants by any of his relief other than probationers whom he insisted, as a matter of policy, should make such an arrest at least once.

The police were aware that they were considered the agency of last resort where vagrants are concerned. Their experience is illustrated by one case described to the researcher independently in almost every interview at Hammersmith: he was described as filthy and gangrenous, his clothes formed part of his skin and he "smelt like a gas leak". He used to sit in the subway at Hammersmith Broadway and "you could see things crawling on him". Although he frequently exposed himself he was never arrested. On one occasion a constable arranged for him to be taken to a Salvation Army hostel but he soon returned. An approach was made to the local social services department but they were powerless to find appropriate services or make him accept them. In the last resort the police felt they had to arrest him in order to provide him with the help he required.

The most usual response to nuisance behaviour on the part of 'vagrants' was to move them on. For example, on one occasion observed, two constables from Bow Street were dispatched to deal with four men (described by the inspector as 'vagrants') causing a disturbance in the vicinity of St Martin's Lane. One of the men was sitting in the middle of the pavement, another two were sitting in a doorway. The fourth walked up staggering slightly. The police inspected a book he was carrying but were satisfied it was not stolen. Three of the men were known to the constables and were sent on their way but a CRO trace was done on the fourth and he was asked to turn out his pockets. Once it was established that the man was not on the wanted index he too was sent on his way.

Few of the homeless persons encountered by the police in Brighton were likely to be lice ridden. Perhaps for this reason there was less expression of distaste at arresting them. Even so the police appeared to minimise their contact with the group of homeless who were well known to them. Their attitude was that they would know where to find them when they required to, for example to execute warrants, so there was little need to bother them unnecessarily. Inspection of the collators' records showed that there was much semi-formal and informal interaction with a group of the homeless who were well known to the police but rarely actually arrested.

The Brighton police not infrequently brought homeless persons into the police station without arresting them, exercising instead their powers under Section 136 of the Mental Health Act, 1959. This empowers the police to take people behaving in a bizarre way or one that endangers themselves or others to 'a place of safety'. They then have to be examined by a doctor who can make a three day detention order. A psychiatrist can subsequently make a 28 day order. A total of eleven persons were taken in by the police using these powers during July 1979. Three of them, two men and a woman, had no fixed address and one of these men was detained twice. During this period extreme difficulty was experienced by the police in having persons certified under a three day order because of union action at the local hospital which affected such admissions. Thus only one three day order was made during July and none of the homeless was compulsorily admitted to hospital. Consequently they were released to return to the streets, a situation which the police considered unsatisfactory.

Complaints from the public

Police interaction with homeless persons appeared to a large extent to be governed by complaints they received from the public. For example, during one period of observation, the police were called to the Bethnal Green Library. A woman vagrant was in the audience of a free film show. The library attendants wanted her removed because her smell was offensive. Two police constables eventually achieved this by talking to the woman and explaining the situation as tactfully as possible. This incident occupied them for more than twenty minutes. On another occasion the management of the Odeon Cinema in Leicester Square sent for the police to move vagrants sheltering in their doorway. There was a total of about twenty individuals in four loose groups, and there were two women in one of the groups. All these individuals moved when requested but none went far away. The police had a word with one of the women, the only person they had not recognised as a regular in the square, but took no further action.

Such complaints appeared however to be relatively infrequent since people who came into contact with vagrants were normally loth to trouble the police, except in extreme cases, and tried to deal with much nuisance behaviour themselves. For example, a car park attendant in Hammersmith reported that vagrants gathered in the doorway opposite the site he supervised. He did not tolerate them on his car park and told them so. He only summoned the police when "things get out of hand". His experience of one such situation was that "the police arrived, arrested some and moved the others on but they were soon back". The researcher was informed that 999 calls were frequently received from the attendants in the toilets at Hammersmith Broadway. The lavatory attendants interviewed, however, had not had occasion to summon the police, but did use the threat of calling them to control the 'winos'. The park keeper in Furnival Gardens, a favourite haunt of the Hammersmith vagrants, had called the police twice in a three month period when they had been causing a nuisance. He reported that the police shifted them but did not arrest them. A park attendant there felt that these vagrants were not much trouble to him. They were, however, a nuisance to other people in the park, frightening women and children, although the park staff received few complaints from the public.

The Brighton police were occasionally called to bed and breakfast hotels catering for the homeless group to deal with violent situations. The researcher was present on one such occasion. Three men shared a room and one of them had been attacked by the two others. The landlord had intervened and only called the police when he failed to calm the situation. There was little the two police officers could do to ensure a satisfactory resolution of the situation other than offer advice to the landlord and speak very firmly to the parties involved.

In all the areas studied the police had to take account of pressures from the commercial sector and these were perhaps stronger in Brighton and around Bow Street, because these areas attracted tourists. The police at Bow Street were also very aware of the local authority's concern. During 1975–76 Westminster City Council convened a working party on 'the problems caused by homeless persons'. This involved the police, St Mungo's and the Highways and Cleansing Departments of the council. The problems considered were:– the offence experienced by shoppers from filth, including material used for bedding; fires lit by the homeless which caused damage to highways; soiling of benches in the parks; and objectional behaviour towards park staff, who frequently had to request police assistance. It was felt, however, that the problem experienced by the council had improved since the working party was set up, due to the co-operation of the police. The police assumed responsibility in that area for moving those sleeping rough from the streets before the council's cleansing vehicles made their daily rounds.

Police contact with agencies assisting the homeless

Discussions both with the police and with agencies providing services for the homeless in each area were designed to discover the amount of contact between them.

The Brighton police made nightly visits to the reception centre to collect 'the lump list', that is the list of residents. They checked the names of any newcomers to see if any individuals were currently wanted and paid particular attention to any anxieties the reception centre staff had about their residents. This relationship appeared to be beneficial to both sides. The police stated that they did occasionally escort people to the reception centre, mainly those homeless not previously known to them or persons with mental problems, and did direct others there. However they were aware that many of the town's regular population of homeless persons are barred from the reception centre. This they considered a problem since it left them no means of finding these individuals shelter. On the other hand, the Brighton police steered clear of the soup run organised nightly by the Brighton Housing Trust, and although they were aware of the hostel they had little or no contact with it.

Although at a senior level there appeared to be fairly good communication between the St. Mungo's Community Trust and the Bow Street police, there was a somewhat uneasy truce between policemen on the beat and the St Mungo's soup run. The soup run was considered to create litter (the debris of paper cups and bread wrappings, although its helpers took great pains to collect all such rubbish before they left) and to attract the dregs of humanity. It was thought that without it the vagrants might help themselves or at least split up into smaller groups and disperse. One inspector suggested that St Mungo's, because it took services to vagrants on the street, was thereby maintaining them in that way of life. The few helpers involved in the soup run to whom the researcher talked appeared to distrust the police. There was, however, contact between police constables and the local authority hostel, Bruce House. This was mainly because the police were so often summoned there to deal with petty offences.

36

The superintendent of Bruce House felt that he was on good terms with the police. He considered that "we have to work with them as we need their assistance in a hurry sometimes". Occasionally the police (mainly those from West End Central station) returned drunken residents to the hostel, and infrequently sent homeless persons there to obtain shelter.

The Community Liaison Officer based at Hammersmith station was on the management committee of a local hostel catering for drug addicts and alcoholics but there was no general contact between police constables and that hostel or any of the others operating locally. One of these, the Riverpoint hostel provided emergency accommodation for up to seven days. It accepted referrals from probation officers and social workers and also took those who turned up on its doorstep. There was virtually no referral from the police because although the project was confident that it could cope with 'anything the police could send' it was already often over occupied and there was no scope for adding the police as a new potential source of referral.

The Detoxification Unit in Booth House, in Bethnal Green's locality, was not a centre approved under Section 34 of the Criminal Justice Act 1972, which provides that a constable can take a person to a treatment centre rather than arresting him or her for an offence of drunkenness. Thus the police felt unable to make direct referrals there. However, the general view encountered was that the provision of more such facilities officially for police use would be beneficial.

Demand for alternative facilities for drunkenness offenders
Drunkenness offenders comprised a large proportion of the homeless petty offenders with whom the police came into contact. Many of these individuals were arrested for their own good rather than for any other reason and thus charging them and processing them through the courts is really inappropriate. Alternative facilities, providing shelter for homeless drunks, while they sobered up, appear to be required in areas where such persons are frequently encountered. All the areas studied would have benefited from such a resource and in Brighton, where a working party was formed to consider the problem of homeless drunken offenders, a proposal was drawn up for establishing a refuge where the police could take drunks and to which drunks could go voluntarily to sober up.

Estimating the demand for such a facility is a complicated problem. The data collected in Brighton were inspected to predict how much use the police might make of a shelter for drunks. The pattern of arrest during July 1979 suggested that the police would not make daily use of it and would probably make two or three referrals on days when they used it and up to six at busy times. The worker who organised the soup run estimated potential voluntary demand as two or three people per night. However, current observations are not a valid basis for predicting demand once a new facility is established: knowledge of its availability might alter the frequency with which the police made arrests. There existed a number of men who were frequently observed by the police when drunk but rarely arrested. These men might be arrested more often if this was construed as a positive action rather than, as currently perceived, a waste of time. Moreover if the shelter was appreciated by its customers, a wider group than that served by the soup run might use it. Indeed there is the risk that some homeless person who would otherwise drift from place to place would stay longer in the town or that an even larger group of homeless individuals might be attracted to Brighton. In short, the provision of new resource might change the behaviour of the police and the homeless.

Conclusion

A proportion of the interactions between the police and petty homeless offenders involved indictable offences which generally speaking allowed no leeway for discretion. Moreover, in situations which permitted discretion the police tended to avoid making arrests where possible, choosing instead to 'move on' the individuals concerned. In each of the areas studied police practice with regard to begging exemplifies this. Arrests were only made when individuals had been abusive or threatening while demanding money or had refused to respond to direct instructions to move from the police.

Drunkenness offences accounted for the majority of arrests of petty homeless offenders and the very fact of an individual's homelessness appeared to reduce the options open to the police when they encountered a person drunk in a public place. Many arrests of homeless persons appeared to have been made for the protection of that individual. A more positive way of catering for these individuals appeared therefore to be required.

In general there was no active use made by the police of facilities for the homeless in their localities. However, while there appeared to be an argument for improving co-operation between the police and existing agencies, this in itself would be unlikely to bring about any major alleviation of the problems faced by the police since the agencies' resources were usually already stretched to their limits. Thus, if the problem posed by homeless drunks is to be dealt with other than by arrest, new facilities will need to be established.

At a basic level, what appears to be needed is simply a shelter to which the police can escort drunks whom they would otherwise charge, where the drunks can sober up under supervision and be allowed to go on their way once they have done so. Discussions with the police during this study suggest that such facilities would be welcomed in localities where homeless people congregate and would indeed reduce the burden at two stages of the criminal justice system, namely, the police stage, where currently time and money are spent in arresting, charging and holding drunks in custody, and at the court stage, where despite the fact that each drunk is dealt with quickly, the numbers to be dealt with in certain areas constitute an onerous load. Since drunkenness offenders cannot be sentenced to imprisonment the provision of such facilities would not have any direct influence on the over-crowding in the prisons. However, given the same drunkenness offenders end up in prison through non-payment of fines there would be an indirect effect that might be fairly substantial in some local prisons.

38

4 Sentencing the persistent petty offender

Introduction

The sentences of imprisonment awarded to persistent petty offenders often appeared out of proportion to the seriousness of the offences they had committed (cf. Chapter 2). However, this probably reflects the fact that magistrates have few alternative options for dealing with these offenders. The study of prisoners in Pentonville demonstrated that an extremely high proportion of those who returned most frequently to prison were homeless, penniless, and lacking any stable base in the community. These factors undoubtedly limited the range of possible sentences. More information, however, was needed about the decision making process in the courts, the range of options actually available to magistrates, and facilities that might be used to bolster these in the case of the homeless.

Two approaches were used to collect information about the current practices of magistrates in dealing with petty persistent offenders – observation by researchers in three magistrates courts and a questionnaire survey. Once these exercises were completed, the findings and their implications for future action discussed with magistrates, justices' clerks and probation officers at the three courts which had co-operated in the observation study. Additionally a series of meetings was arranged with members of the Treatment of Offenders Committee of the Magistrates' Association to consider what extra facilities would be desirable to avoid such sentencing problems in respect of persistent petty offenders.

The questionnaire survey

The survey covered a four week period during Spring 1979. Twenty-two courts, which provided a wide spread across a variety of environments and different parts of the country, were invited to take part in the questionnaire survey. Six declined to take part. The courts participating included two in city areas, six in predominantly urban areas (one of which did not send in any returns) and eight which served both urban and rural areas (five of which made nil returns).

A questionnaire was to be completed for every petty persistent offender, aged 30 or over, sentenced during the relevant period. Persistent offenders were defined as those with 'at least four previous convictions (at least one in the previous eighteen months)'. The notes accompanying the questionnaire deliberately did not specify 'petty offences' suggesting that "the details of the offence rather than its category determine whether or not it can be classified as petty"

39

and requested that, if there was doubt as to whether any individual fell within the criteria, they be included. The courts were also asked to be flexible over the age criterion if an individual appeared otherwise to fall within the remit, and returns for those aged 25 and over were actually included in the analysis. The particular concern of this research with offenders who were homeless and lacking stable community ties was explained.

The main object of the exercise was to discover whether magistrates were satisfied that the sentences they awarded to petty persistent offenders were really appropriate. Magistrates were asked to fill in rating scales to show how satisfied they were with the sentences awarded in each case and to give their suggestions for an ideal disposal for each individual (regardless of whether existing facilities or legislation actually permitted it).

The number of forms completed about individual offenders was suprisingly low in view of the impression previously gained from magistrates about the burden put on their courts by this type of offender. As previously noted, six courts did not find a single case fitting the criteria during the four weeks and (excluding cases not fitting the criteria) only 58 cases were received from the other ten courts. Half of these were returned from the two courts in city areas.

All but four of the cases were men; their average age was 49, 15 being 50 or older. Thirty-nine (67 per cent) were unemployed at the time of their court appearance and only nine were in regular employment, 21 (36 per cent) were of no fixed abode (ie living in a hostel, common lodging house or sleeping rough), 11 (19 per cent) were either in a bedsit or were in lodgings or were living with relatives or friends (considered as having a temporary home) and 26 (45 per cent) had a permanent home.

The average number of previous convictions among the 55 for whom this information was available was 15. The main charge against 26 of the cases was theft (in 12 of these cases shoplifting was involved) and another 13 were charged with other property offences; nine were charged with offences against the person, four with offences under the Vagrancy Act, 1824, and five with drunkenness offences. Details of the charge were missing in one case. (More drunkenness offences might have been expected, but one of the city courts did not complete forms in respect of such charges because they felt it would have created too much work.)

All but six pleaded guilty. A social inquiry report was presented to the court for 26 cases (43 per cent) and 32 (55 per cent) were legally represented. Only defendants for whom SIRs had been prepared were made the subject of a probation order. All but three of those who were sent to prison were legally represented. None of the nine appearing on charges under the vagrancy acts or of drunkenness were legally represented and only for two of them were social inquiry reports prepared. Nineteen of the defendants were fined (from £1 to £260), twelve were sentenced to immediate imprisonment (with terms varying from 14 days to 12 months) and another nine were awarded suspended prison sentences, six were put on probation and three were ordered to do community service; seven were conditionally discharged and another two discharged absolutely.

In response to the question about the appropriateness of the sentences actually awarded there were 35 (60 per cent) answers of satisfied, 11 (19 per cent) of fairly satisfied, four (7 per cent) of fairly dissatisfied and eight (24 per cent) of dissatisfied.

Table 7 shows their satisfaction with the various types of sentence.

Table 7
Magistrates' satisfaction with sentence awarded

Sentence	Satisfied	Fairly satisfied	Fairly dissatisfied/ dissatisfied	Total
Imprisonment	7	1	5	13
Fine	10	5	4	19
Suspended sentence	6	3		9
Probation	5	1		6
Community service order	2			2
Conditional/absolute discharge	3		2	5
Sentence not specified	2	1	1	4
Total	35	11	12	58

In 54 per cent of cases where imprisonment was awarded, in 53 per cent of fines and 72 per cent of other non-custodial sentences, the magistrates were satisfied with the sentence. They were fairly dissatisfied or dissatisfied with 38 per cent of the sentences to imprisonment and 21 per cent of the fines, but with only 9 per cent of other non-custodial sentences. Their satisfaction with the sentences awarded was related to the defendant's accommodation. They tended to be satisfied where the defendant had a permanent or temporary home but were much less likely to be satisfied if the defendant had no fixed abode, as Table 8 indicates.

Table 8
Magistrates' satisfaction and accommodation

Accommodation	Satisfied	Fairly satisfied	Fairly dissatisfied/ dissatisfied	Total
Permanent home	21	4	1	26
Temporary home	5	5	1	11
No fixed abode	9	2	10	21
Total	35	11	12	58

Magistrates were asked to comment on their level of satisfaction with the sentence actually awarded and to suggest the disposal they would have liked to have given. In the majority of cases the magistrates were satisfied to a greater or lesser extent and had no suggestions for alternatives. However, their comments illustrated some of the factors that influenced their decision. For example, an unemployed man aged 51, living in a common lodging house, was sentenced to a month's imprisonment for shoplifting. He had 13 previous convictions six of them in the past three years and had last appeared in court less than a month previously when he was given a suspended sentence on another charge of theft. This last factor determined the disposal on this occasion. Another bench was satisfied with a fine of £1 or one day's imprisonment (which would be counted as served by the time the court rose) in the case of a man aged 52, again unemployed and living in a common lodging house, charged with wilfully obstructing the highway. They commented, however, that the offence was 'harmless' and that a police warning would have been sufficient.

The comments sometimes revealed that the magistrates had considered an alternative sentence but rejected it. For example, in the case of a 59 year old man with 24 previous convictions, given a suspended sentence for dishonestly using electricity and theft of property worth £10 belonging to the Electricity Board, the magistrates commented, "community service is available but not a suitable scheme for this sort of man who is really an idle drunkard".

In four cases the suggestion made for an 'ideal' sentence was for a specific alternative that should have been available according to the replies given in the part of the survey that asked about facilities. One of these defendants, a homeless man aged 31 with nine previous convictions, was appearing on a charge of criminal damage, breaking a window in order to sleep in a school. A factor that influenced the magistrates was that he had been admitted to one mental hospital on 12 occasions since 1969, diagnosed as a schizophrenic. They would have liked to have made a hospital order under the Mental Health Act 1959, but after considerable enquiry were unable to achieve this. He was eventually awarded a month's imprisonment, a sentence which the magistrates considered "disgraceful". In another case a bench was faced with a 36 year old defendant charged with behaviour likely to cause a breach of the peace. He had been arrested for masturbating in a public toilet, and had sex offences in his record. Again, they would have liked to have ordered psychiatric treatment, but instead they fined him. In two cases appearing before another court the magistrates would have liked to have awarded probation with a condition of residence. Both these defendants had been sleeping rough. One of them, aged 43, with 45 previous convictions, was charged with travelling on the railway without paying the fare and was sentenced to two months imprisonment, which was considered entirely unsatisfactory. The other was 57 and had seven previous convictions. He was charged with theft of a bar of chocolate and was discharged absolutely. It was noted that this defendant "refuses to accept probation" so even had a probation hostel place been available the court would have not been able to take advantage of it.

In two cases the bench wished to use a combination of a suspended sentence and probation which is not available to the magistrates' court – although it can be imposed by the crown court in the form of a suspended sentence supervision order. One of these cases involved a man aged 43 who already had 11 convictions. He had recently served a prison sentence and was in temporary accommodation. In court he stated that he was willing to be placed on probation, although this contradicted an earlier statement to the probation officer who presented a social inquiry report. He was charged with shoplifting (pork chops worth 85½p from a supermarket) and was also sentenced for a previous conviction for theft and deception for which sentence had been deferred. The total sentence was 12 months imprisonment suspended for two years.

The magistrates' comments occasionally revealed sheer frustration at their lack of control over defendants. One example was an old lady of 74 charged with shoplifting. She had seven previous convictions and was already on probation. She lived in her own home. The case had been adjourned for investigation of accommodation in an old persons' home, but eventually she refused to go there. She was fined £5 and the magistrates commented "We should have liked to do something to keep her away from shops but were unable to do anything constructive".

Where magistrates were less than satisfied their suggestion for ideal sentences frequently involved the notion of compulsory treatment or long term institutional care. The following three examples illustrate this:

A man, aged 35 with numerous previous convictions who was sleeping rough at arrest, was charged with being drunk and disorderly and failure to surrender to bail. He was fined £25 to be paid at £1 per week or seven days imprisonment. The magistrates commented that this was a quite unsuitable case for a fine and the prison sentence "will do no good". They would have liked to have sent him to "an inebriates' home for containment or cure".

A man, aged 62, with 42 previous convictions, who was in a probation hostel at arrest, was charged with two offences of burglary, 14 other offences being taken into consideration. He was sentenced to six months imprisonment. The magistrates noted that his longest period at liberty during the past 46 years was five months and that his offences had been committed within days of release from prison. He was said to be institutionalised and unable to cope with life outside prison so the bench would have preferred "to have placed him in a home with strict supervision".

A man, aged 68, with 'many' previous convictions (11 in the past three years), sleeping rough at arrest, was charged with theft of socks and imprisoned. The magistrates felt that prison was "not really appropriate although expected to go there" but they considered "the public needed protection". Their ideal suggestion was "a sort of secure home for rogues".

The observation study
Birmingham, Coventry and Oxford were the locations chosen for the other two parts of this exercise, namely observation in magistrates courts and gathering information about facilities for the homeless and for those with alcohol

related problems. These areas were selected because published Criminal Statistics[1] indicated that they dealt with a substantial number of the type of offender with which the research was concerned; Thames Valley police force (covering Oxford) dealt with more offences of begging and sleeping out than any force apart from the Metropolitan Police District, and the West Midlands ranked third (after the MPD and Greater Manchester) for charges of drunkenness.

When planning the exercise it had been intended that, at the end of each morning's sitting, the researchers would meet with one or more of the magistrates to discuss the factors that the magistrates had considered in passing sentence and how satisfied they were with those sentences. This was based on the asssumption that during a single morning in one court room a number of relevant cases would have been dealt with. In the event this assumption was not borne out. Cases falling within the remit were few and far between (a finding which bore out the experience of the questionnaire study) and it was decided instead to meet with groups of magistrates and others from the three courts after the preliminary stage of the research to discuss the findings.

The observation study was planned to cover a week's sittings at each of the courts (spread over a longer period because of other research commitments). Table 9 shows the number of sessions observed and that this resulted in only nine cases being identified by the researchers as relevant. The researchers sat in court rooms which dealt (among other cases) with overnight arrests because it was expected that they would pick up more relevant cases there. However, this selection resulted in a bias towards drunkenness offences and a preponderance of cases dealt with at first appearance.

Table 9
Sessions observed and cases identified

Court	No. of different days	No. of sessions observed	Total cases identified as relevant	Drunkenness offences	Other offences
Birmingham	6	11	5	4	1
Coventry	6	9	2	2	–
Oxford	5	8	2	–	2
Total	17	28	9	6	3

The nine cases in fact relate to eight defendants as one offender was observed on two separate occasions in Coventry Magistrates' Court.

All the defendants were male, their ages ranged from 27 to 47 (36 on average). All were unemployed. Three were recorded as being of no fixed abode, one lived in lodgings, one in a bedsit, two with their parents and one had an address

---

[1] Criminal Statistics England and Wales 1975. Table XIII Persons proceeded against for non-indictable offences: by police-force area and offence.

in his own right. These last three might be considered as having settled addresses but were included because their home situations were tenuous by virtue of unemployment and drink problems. All the defendants pleaded guilty and for only two were social inquiry reports presented to the court. Of the defendants appearing at Birmingham three were charged with simple drunkenness. Two, who appeared together, were fined £20 each and the third £15. Another was charged with being drunk and disorderly. He was fined £15 for this offence and was ordered to pay this fine and another £131 on outstanding warrants at £3 per week. The final defendant observed was charged with criminal damage (he broke a glass valued at £3.25 the property of his ex-girlfriend's new boy-friend) and was conditionally discharged for one year.

Records showed that the individual identified at Coventry made frequent court appearances. The researchers first observed him on 10 April when he was fined £3 for being drunk and incapable. Between 25 May and 17 July he was charged with five drunkenness offences and on each occasion was fined £1 with the alternative of 1 days imprisonment. He failed to answer to bail twice in this period. At the appearance covered by the study on 4 June, when he was charged with being drunk and disorderly and failure to surrender for bail, his case was adjourned for preparation of a social inquiry report. Eventually on 17 July he was fined £1 on the first count and sentenced to 3 months imprisonment on the second count. This prison term was extended by the imposition of another 3 months sentence for two other offences of failure to appear.

Of the two defendants at Oxford one was charged with being drunk and incapable and was fined £10, while the other was charged with using insulting words and behaviour and fined £25 or seven days. Discussions with the probation service suggested that the sessions observed by the researchers had been atypical in that only one drunkenness offender of no fixed abode and no defendants charged with begging, had appeared. To supplement the observation, therefore, court lists for July were inspected. During that month one defendant (a male, aged 63) had appeared three times charged with begging, on two of these occasions he was fined £5 and on the third was detained to the rising of the court. Eleven defendants were, between them, due to have made 30 appearances for drunkenness. One of these offenders was a woman aged 38. The men's ages ranged from 22 to 72 but the majority of them were over 40 years old. On more than a third of the occasions the defendants failed to appear. The usual penalty for simple drunkenness was a £10 fine but the woman was awarded a six month probation order for two such offences. For being drunk and disorderly defendants were fined sums from £15 to £50.

Although only one of the defendants identified was sentenced to immediate imprisonment others may well have eventually been committed to prison, and indeed one of the defendants observed was imprisoned for seven days forthwith since he could not pay the fine of £25 imposed. In other cases where defendants failed to pay fines, more costs were likely to be incurred by the police and courts in executing warrants either for further court appearances, when alternatives for non-payment had not been set, or for committal to prison.

The survey of facilities

The aim of the survey of facilities was to collect information about all the resources available that catered for the homeless and for problem drinkers in the three localities, and to comment on whether the courts could use them more extensively. It was initially planned with a view to suggesting ways in which existing facilities could be used to avoid imprisonment of persistent petty offenders by the three courts observed. In the event only a single sentence of immediate imprisonment of relevant offenders was picked up in the courts' study. However, fining persistent petty offenders often results in their committal to prison, so facilities which could be called upon in order to use a probation order as a realistic non-custodial alternative still appear relevant to the study.

The facilities discovered in each area were known to the local probation services which in turn were in contact with fairly large numbers of the homeless. In Oxford and Coventry specific officers catered for the homeless, and Birmingham had recently appointed an ancillary worker as an accommodation officer to provide assistance for this group. Although in many cases when a homeless petty persistent offender appeared in the courts the probation and after-care service were involved informally, few such offenders were subject to probation orders.

The areas studied appeared relatively well endowed with facilities for the homeless. Birmingham and Coventry both had a range of accommodation but, in both cities, the supply of hostel places was insufficient to meet the demand and there were substantial numbers sleeping rough. Oxford had a night shelter but appeared to lack second stage accommodation to which night shelter users could progress. In Oxford there appeared to be reasonably good access to alcoholism treatment for the homeless through either the probation and after-care service or the social services. The services available were a five day detoxification programme and a three week treatment programme. Birmingham also had a range of treatment facilities for alcoholics and addicts (although these did not seem readily available to the group the research was concerned with) but Coventry lacked any such resources. Coventry's Norton day centre appeared to be a relevant and useful facility. Run by a voluntary trust it operated an open door policy to cater for the city's homeless and provided showers, laundry facilities, free soup and tea and a range of activities. The probation officer designated to work with the homeless was based there. The Oxford probation and after-care service ran a day centre on a small scale and there was one run by the local authority in Birmingham, but these facilities needed supplementing in order to provide a more comprehensive service.

Although gaps in available facilities were noted in all the three cities, there appeared to be a sufficient basis for more effort to be made by the courts to settle some of the homeless petty offenders, or at least to maintain them in the community without recourse to imprisonment. There appeared to be scope for making more extensive use of the existing facilities, which might be achieved through the greater involvement both formally and informally, of the probation and after-care service.

Further discussions with magistrates
The preliminary stages of this study did not provide a basis for proceeding immediately to action research. The size of the sample used for the questionnaire study was very small and the observational study was even more limited. Its main findings tended to be in opposition to one another. On the one hand the results suggested that magistrates were in general satisfied with their sentencing decisions, even when awarding imprisonment. They were least likely to be satisfied when the offender was homeless but their dissatisfaction was more likely to stem from being unable to impose heavier penalties than from having limited options for non-custodial alternatives. They appeared to incline to the view that such offenders were suffering from 'personality disorders' or 'alcoholism' and should be sentenced so as to ensure both their removal from society and their compulsory treatment. These findings were disappointing since a way of minimizing contact between petty persistent offenders and the criminal justice system was being sought. On the other hand, however, there was room for some optimism in that the survey of facilities suggested that the three areas were reasonably well endowed with resources for the homeless, and that there appeared to be scope for making more extensive use of them in order to keep offenders out of prison. Further discussions were, accordingly, arranged with representatives of the magistrates and the probation service at Birmingham, Coventry and Oxford.

The questionnaire survey had identified two distinct groups, a relatively small group of homeless people whose offending stemmed mainly from the situation they experienced and a larger group, mainly younger persons, who appeared more deliberately antisocial. In the case of younger offenders there was hope that intervention could effect change; but in the case of older persons there was no place for such optimism and the problem appeared to be one of how to make continuing provision. It was the older, homeless group that was the subject of the discussions. There was a tendency to concentrate on drunkenness offending, but it was acknowledged that the group under consideration, who appeared frequently in court, were charged with a wide range of offences.

During the course of discussions the hard line attitude that had emerged from the questionnaire survey was stated. It was felt that there were strong reasons why members of the group should be removed from the community; namely, in order to protect the public (one magistrate who expressed this view considered that the "hard core of incurable beggars" was "a menace to the community"); to give a rest to the police, courts and probation service who had to deal with them so frequently; and to remove the offenders from their environment as a necessary condition for them to change their drinking habits. However, this point of view was countered by other magistrates who were keen to explore ways of containing homeless petty offenders in the community.

There was a general feeling that awarding one day's imprisonment as an alternative to a fine was a misuse of the court's powers and that punishment was in many cases inappropriate. There was therefore a need to divert many drunkenness offenders prior to their coming to court. The Leeds detoxification centre was overwhelmingly considered a positive resource and the magistrates urged the provision of more such facilities.

The group was uniformly perceived by the magistrates to have chronic drink problems. There was discussion of the disadvantages to the system of cash grants given by the Department of Health and Social Security and by prisons at the point of discharge. Abuses of the system by men who squandered these sums on drink were chronicled. The consensus was that it would be better for the state to issue vouchers for full board and to recognise that residual cash would normally be spent on alcohol. However, it was recognised that there were problems concerning individuals' rights and paternalism inherent in this suggestion.

It was acknowledged that the probation and after-care service had a key role in keeping homeless petty offenders out of prison. The magistrates tended to have a mis-conception of the probation and after-care services' readiness to be involved with this type of offender and the discussions tended to correct this as the probation and after-care service representatives present were able to reassure them of the general willingness to prepare reports for the court in respect of homeless offenders and to accept them on probation.

In reviewing existing facilities and outlining new plans for developments, the discussions emphasised that day centres are potentially useful resources in enabling homeless petty offenders to be diverted from prison, and even from the criminal justice system altogether. Through such resources, the probation and after-care service is able to keep in contact with homeless offenders. It can thus present the court with viable recommendations and maintain its credibility. However, for a day centre to operate successfully it needs to be complemented by a network of accommodation and treatment facilities.

Suggestions from the Magistrates' Association
Meetings with members of the Magistrates' Association were held at various stages during this study and were valuable in its development. The sub-committee concerned made its own independent appraisal of the sort of provision that would be desirable to overcome the problems faced in sentencing petty persistent offenders. Such provision it was hoped, would lead to "a reduction in the numbers of those attracting prison sentences".

The recommendations made in the paper prepared by members of the Magistrates' Association paralleled closely the disadvantages identified among the Pentonville sample of petty persistent offenders. The magistrates pointed to the need for "provision of hostels and sheltered accommodation; voluntary and statutory, large and small, some with warden some on a less formal bedsit basis" noting their opinion that "it is only by the provision of the widest possible variety of accommodation that there can be any hope of meeting some of the men and women's needs". It was suggested that sheltered workshops or small centres offering training in everyday and social skills could be run in conjunction with hostels. The magistrates felt that "given accommodation and support [these offenders] might . . . well be able to undertake community service as an alternative to a prison sentence".

The magistrates felt that accommodation and workshop provision should be available to a wider group than just recent offenders noting that "it may be easier to re-integrate the ex-prisoner if he is not segregated in a labelled ex-offender community". This point is one that is now becoming widely endorsed involving a move towards the provision of 'open door' facilities wherever feasible.

The magistrates recognised that members of the group presented special problems, among them personality disorder, drug abuse and drink problems. With regard to the latter their report noted, "the provision of more detoxification centres with adequate back-up facilities remains an urgent need. Smaller alcoholic treatment units . . . with after-care hostel facilities should also be seen as a valuable alternative to a prison sentence for some offenders with alcoholic problems".

A new approach was suggested to cope with the problem of making "continuing provision for the persistent petty offender recidivist", namely "an experimental unit attached to one of the major prisons to which prisoners [including those serving short sentences] could be transferred during their sentences". "They would be entitled to stay on after their date of release and to return if they failed to settle outside". A number of problems would need to be resolved in order to pursue such an experiment and it is unlikely that the resources necessary to its running would be available during the foreseeable future.

The paper made very important points about the need for co-ordination of provisions and for the accessibility of relevant information. On this it stated "in order to make the best possible use of the widely dispersed and fragmented facilities that are available, it would be desirable to have a contact point in the major urban areas where rootless ex-offenders are to be found". This could be a shop front or other centre manned by volunteers and "where if at all possible sleeping accommodation might also be provided" for emergency use.

49

Conclusions

In order for alternative decisions to be made at the point of sentence it seems that two conditions have to be changed. First, the provision of support services to the group of persistent petty offenders it is wished to contain in the community (principally the older, homeless recidivists) needs to be strengthened. Secondly, magistrates have to adopt a more tolerant attitude to their offending and develop confidence in the community's ability to cope with them as individuals. The probation and after-care service appears to have a key role in meeting both of these conditions. On the one hand they can take a hand in co-ordinating the facilities that already exist to cater for this group and on the other they can influence magistrates by presenting social inquiry reports to the court which offer viable alternatives to custodial sentences.

Day centres which figured recurrently in discussions with magistrates and others appear to be a promising resource in enabling the probation and after-care service to contain homeless persistent petty offenders in the community. Such centres can provide a day time refuge for persons who otherwise have to resort to the streets and public places to fill empty hours and to find companionship. By providing basic facilities such as showers, somewhere to shave and to launder clothing, they enable the homeless to maintain themselves at a reasonable standard; and the provision of free tea and cheap meals may encourage persons to avoid daytime drinking. At the same time day centres may allow probation officers to maintain contact with a group who would otherwise not report to them.

The day centre can also become the nucleus of co-ordinated resources. Backed up by a network of other support facilities offering, for example, accommodation, treatment for drink problems and sheltered work, they may allow for positive intervention in cases where this is feasible and, in cases where continuing support is required, can also cater appropriately. Thus, day centres appear to give the probation and after-care service a viable basis for containing petty persistent offenders in the community, one that they can present to the courts as a feasible way of substantially reducing the prison population.

5 The Pentonville project

Introduction
The point of discharge from prison was the only decision point at which it was possible to proceed immediately to an action project. In a sense intervention at this point comes too late to alleviate the burden on the criminal justice system. However, the provision of extra welfare resources and support on release from prison is intended to give persistent petty offenders better opportunities on their return into the community, and this might delay their typically rapid return to prison. The initial descriptive study indicated that chronic ϒ homelessness was a prevalent disadvantage among the group serving short sentences for trivial offences and an invariable characteristic of those identified as the core group in both samples aged 30 and over. Homelessness also appeared ⟩ to be the one problem among the four areas of disadvantage which that study selected (the others being employment, social isolation and drink problems) that could be appropriately tackled. Thus the Pentonville project was designed to help homeless prisoners find accommodation to go to on release.

Establishing the project
The project appeared to fit naturally into the work of Pentonville's welfare liaison unit. As noted in Chapter 2 this unit dealt with almost all welfare matters for men sentenced to three months or less. Ever since it was originally set up in 1972 the unit had been involved in finding both accommodation and employment for prisoners on release. Over the years it had, however, gained other responsibilities so that it could only play a limited role in securing accommodation. Its only resource in this respect was that of the Catholic social services, the representative of which visited Pentonville weekly. In the case of men serving short sentences, he was rarely able to arrange accommodation in advance and although he invited men to call at his office on release, when he would secure hostel accommodation for them, few actually took up his offer.

At the time of the descriptive study of Pentonville's petty persistent offenders in 1977 there had been two probation officers detailed to the welfare liaison unit. However, with the appointment of an assistant governor, responsible for forward planning, management and development of the unit, they were withdrawn so that when this project was planned the unit was staffed only by prison officers. Moreover, due to a general shortage of manpower, its staff were frequently detailed to other duties resulting on occasion in its complete closure. The situation was such that the welfare liaison unit, as constituted, could not possibly take on any extra work. A principal prison officer was therefore assigned to the welfare liaison unit specifically to undertake the project for a three month period commencing on 24 January 1972. His posting was later extended by six weeks to 31 May 1979.

Prior to the commencement of the project, discussions took place with the Inner London Probation and After-Care Service (ILPAS) about access to after-care hostels and the possible involvement of probation service voluntary associates in the project. It was agreed that the project would notify the senior probation officers who were responsible as liaison officers for hostels in the Inner London area whenever a placing was made to any of their hostels. ILPAS agreed to recruit volunteers for the project through the Society of Voluntary Associations and to support them.

The task
The task facing the project was defined as comprising three elements:

   i establishing contacts with a range of hostels and related facilities and persuading them to accept referrals from Pentonville;

   ii persuading individual prisoners to accept help in booking accommodation of a higher standard than they could find for themselves; and

   iii providing support and encouragement for the men to take up the places arranged for them and to settle there on release.

Establishing contacts
The project officer started to make contacts with hostels and other facilities before the project officially started and he continued to extend the network throughout. It was important to have access to accommodation all over London and to be able to call on different types and standards of accommodation. The facilities contacted therefore ranged widely and included a housing association, bed and breakfast hotels, transport hotels and emergency night shelters, as well as hostels and common lodging houses.

In general hostel wardens and managers seemed sympathetic to the project. However many of them laid down conditions which effectively rules out a large proportion of the men the project was concerned with. Some hostels would not take anyone with a drink problem; others would take only men who genuinely intended to stop drinking. Although it had been intended not to include the lowest level of provision in the projects' network, in the event these were found to be necessary to it, partly because some men wished to go on release to places they already knew and partly because it was impossible to place some men in better facilities without the project losing its credibility with those resources.

The following breakdown shows the types of accommodation facilities (29 establishments in total) that were contacted and those that were used during the project. In many cases the after-care and specialist hostels did not have vacancies when the project required places and a couple such hostels declined to accept some of the men referred.

Table 10
Accommodation facilities contacted and used during the project

Type of facility	Contacted	Used
After-care hostels (grant aided)	8	6
Other specialist hostels	5	1
DHSS reception centres	4	4
Common lodging houses	8	2
Bed and breakfast etc hotels	1	1
Emergency shelters	2	1
Housing associations	1	1
Total	29	16

One particularly helpful arrangement was made with the Department of Health and Social Security reception centres, to obtain access to the smaller more select centres directly from Pentonville. Previously it had been necessary for men wishing to go to these centres to go first to the Gordon Road reception centre. This was a demoralising experience involving inspection for infestation and a compulsory bath – even where unneccessary as in the case of those arriving straight from prison in a fresh suit of clothes. By-passing Gordon Road was therefore a welcome achievement.

Contact was also made with day time facilities. Many men in this group needed somewhere to go to pass the time without having to resort to pubs or to open air drinking for company and distraction. The North Lambeth day centre and the two 'shop fronts' run by the Alcoholics Recovery Project (ARP) as advice centres and general meeting places for homeless alcoholics were alternatives open to men with drinking problems. Workers from the ARP also become involved in supporting and motivating men in the project.

The Peter Bedford Trust was approached during the search for accommodation and this led to an unanticipated development. The Trust's main purpose is to provide work through its registered company John Bellairs Ltd, and it was agreed that prisoners from Pentonville would be taken on to work part-time during the last part of their sentence. During the period of the project only one man participated in this scheme. He went out from Pentonville on two days each week for four weeks and continued to work for the company for three weeks after release, even though he disappeared from his hostel place after only a few days.

The National Association for Voluntary Hostels was another useful contact. They were very willing for Pentonville to make use of their free placing service.

The project officer sought their assistance mainly when men wished to go out of London on release and in cases where his own efforts had produced no results. They were usually able to offer a hostel place.

Contacting the 'no fixed address' group

A high proportion of those received into Pentonville are recorded as having 'no fixed address'. In a sixteen week period during the project, the reception figures showed that 30 per cent of the 2,714 men received from court to start their sentences (including fine defaulters and civil prisoners) were 'NFA'.

For the feasibility study it was decided to restrict the group to be included to those sentenced without the option of a fine for terms of between one month and three months inclusive. One month was thought to be the minimum period needed for the project to make accommodation arrangements. These criteria thus covered men who were the responsibility of the welfare liason unit and who would be in receipt of the NFA discharge grant on release. (Civil prisoners and fine defaulters are not eligible for such a grant.) The group was also limited to those who would be received and released during the period of the project so that as the end of the project approached only men serving shorter and shorter terms could be included.

One hundred and twenty five men who were identified as fitting these criteria attended for an interview with the project officer, four of them on two separate sentences. At the first interview men were asked about the sort of accommodation recently used and how long they had been without a settled address; about their employment and source of income; and about their criminal record (ie how many convictions and terms of imprisonment they had had, and when they were last released from prison). The project officer attempted to discover whether they would like help in finding accommodation without raising expectations he might not be able to fulfil. By the end of the interview the project officer would decide whether to take any further action and, if he did so, could start to search for a suitable place.

A sizeable number of the men interviewed maintained that they needed no help. In some cases this was because they felt they were able to find acceptable accommodation for themselves, although the project officer did not usually think that they were. In other cases men appeared satisfied with the common lodging house accommodation open to them or were resigned to skippering or living rough, not being prepared to modify their drinking habits. Some were not prepared to pay for accommodation in advance, one of the conditions of the project. Many men who declined help at the first interview were seen again, but only a few changed their original decision.

Of those who wanted accommodation, some were found accommodation and others could not be helped. The common reasons for being unable to help men were that they wished to go to specific addresses which had no vacancies or which refused the individual concerned or that their drinking habits were such that no hostel or common lodging house would find them acceptable so that the project would alienate its network by trying to place them. Men in this situation were given a list of addresses to try on release. Three men were not able to be helped by the project because they were transferred from Pentonville before arrangements could be made and two because they were to remain in custody awaiting trial once their current sentences were finished.

In some cases the project officer made a specific arrangement but the individual concerned refused it. Some hostels insisted on interviewing men prior to release, to assess their suitability. Four men declined the places offered to them after they had been interviewed in Pentonville by someone from the hostel. One man was granted a few hours temporary release to visit a hostel, he accepted and subsequently settled down well there. In order to have the accommodation arrangement finalised, a prisoner had to sign a form authorising the deduction of one week's rent (usually between £10 and £20 depending on type of board provided) from his NFA discharge grant of £35. Although this had previously been agreed to, some men changed their minds at this point, usually after signing the agreement. At the beginning of the project, this twice caused difficulties for the project officer who had to try to restore money already transferred. Subsequently he allowed more time to elapse before acting on the men's authorisations.

Men seen during the project
For the purpose of analysing information about the men interviewed, they were assigned to one of four 'requirement categories' according to the outcome of the interview with the project officer and his subsequent action. Of the four men interviewed twice during the project, three were unable to be placed on either occasion and the other was found accommodation to his first sentence and was unable to be placed on the second and was assigned to 'placed in accommodation' for analysis.

They fell into the four categories as follows:

declined help	55
unable to be placed	30
rejected specific offer	8
placed in accommodation	32

There was little difference between the groups in terms of relevant characteristics such as age, accommodation history and previous criminal record.

The project catered for all age groups but only a quarter of those seen were aged less than 30. The average age of all those included in the project was 41 and those who declined help tended to be slightly younger than the rest. There were no differences between men in the different requirement categories in the type of accommodation they had been using previously nor the length of time they had been of no fixed address. Prior to arrest, 18 of the men had been sleeping rough, 44 had been living in a squat or skipper (ie in derelict premises), 34 had been in a reception centre, hostel or common lodging house, 19 had been in bedsitters, lodgings or hotels and six living with friends or relatives. No information was recorded about four men's accommodation. Sixty-seven men had had no fixed address for over five years and only 19 had been homeless for less than a year. Thirty-two men seen during the project had been born in Scotland and 24 in Ireland; 21 had been born in London; 39 in the rest of England and Wales and nine abroad. There were fewer Scots and more Londoners in the group who did not require any assistance. Seventy four of the men were considered by the project officer to have a drink problem, but they were no more prevalent in one of the requirement categories than another.

There were no differences in the lengths of sentences being served by men in the different categories nor in the offences they had committed, the great majority of those seen being charged with theft. From their own accounts, 73 of them had last been released from prison less than a year previously, 15 of them within the last month. However, in this respect those who declined help differed from the rest, half of them had not been in prison for at least a year compared to only 22 per cent of the rest.

Information about previous criminal records came from the men's own accounts and CRO records. The two sources of information gave much the same impression but the men themselves often claimed more offences than their records noted which was probably due to offences of drunkenness not being notified to Scotland Yard. In order to show more accurately the burden these men put on the criminal justice system the higher number was counted for each individual. Only 14 men had fewer than six previous convictions while 58 had more than 20. Nine men had never been to prison previously (and another two had only been in prison on remand), while 40 had more than 10 previous prison terms. According to CRO records which were available for 119 of these interviewed, 41 men had each been sentenced to a total of more than four years in prison and 21 to more than 10 years. While there were no differences between the criminal records of men in the different requirement categories in the above respects, those placed in accommodation tended to have been older when they started to offend.

Support and motivation
In addition to making arrangements for accommodation, the project also aimed at encouraging men to settle into a more conventional way of life on release. Thus, as well as dealing with practicalities, the interviews with the project officer also served to influence the men to look realistically at the situation they would face on release. The project officer was able to offer both moral support and practical advice. For example, he could suggest ways in which they could occupy their time, discuss their drinking problems, advise on where to seek help, and ensure that they knew how to claim their entitlement to benefit or pensions.

It seemed likely that more support would be necessary to ensure successful transition from prison to a settled life in the community and it was for this reason that probation volunteers were involved in the project. The original intention was that every man for whom the project made an accommodation arrangement would be given the chance of being linked with an individual volunteer. The volunteer would meet the man in prison prior to his release on at least one occasion, preferably more, would meet him at the prison gate on the day of his release, would accompany him to his accommodation and there provide company and also help him settle in, by introducing him to the warden and staff, helping him sort out arrangements with the local Social Security, office and helping with shopping. After the initial commitment, contact between the man and the volunteer would depend on the two people involved, but it was hoped that the volunteer would attempt to keep in touch to provide practical assistance and company.

This aim was never realised and the involvement of volunteers in the project was disappointing. Even before the project began, it was anticipated that the men would be unlikely to request to be linked with volunteers whom they had never met. For this reason it was decided to hold group sessions of roughly equal numbers of volunteers and prisoners. Each weekly session was split into two parts, a period of one-to-one conversation between pairs of volunteers and prisoners followed by a general discussion on a topic such as 'how to spend time when unemployed'. The group met on five occasions after which it was discontinued because it failed to fulfil any of the purposes envisaged. The same prisoners had attended on each occasion and only one of these men wished to be met by a volunteer after release. Although the volunteers and prisoners got on well in individual conversation, the group discussions failed, partly because the life style of the prisoners was so far from anything the volunteers had ever experienced.

It was decided to concentrate instead on one-to-one contacts and providing an escorting service. However, even escorts were only used on three occasions, and in only two cases did the volunteer (at his own suggestion) meet the man beforehand. The two volunteers concerned felt that the service they provided was welcomed by the men but there was no further contact after arrival at the accommodation address. Another of the volunteers wrote to one of the prisoners who had been in the group meetings offering to meet him after release but he received no reply.

One reason for the little use made of the volunteers was resistance on the part of the project officer who was unwilling to run the risk of an unduly burdensome relationship being formed. Since the group of volunteers had been formed especially for the project, there was no existing support from the probation and after-care service, and this exacerbated his anxiety.

The project's co-operation with the Alcoholics Recovery Project to provide support was much more promising. In this case the project worker was confident that the ARP's social workers were already aware of what the prisoners would be like and that the organisation could cope with any extreme. Contact between Pentonville and the ARP extended to a wider group than that covered by the project. An ARP social worker visited individual men and, towards the end of the feasibility period, arrangements were made for the ARP to hold group sessions to discuss problem drinking and explain what the ARP could offer. The men invited to attend included some already well known to the ARP and others who were likely to be homeless in South London on release and therefore potential users. The first of the sessions, tried as an experiment, was felt to have been useful and further meetings were arranged.

The outcome

Thirty two men had accommodation arranged for them and Table 11 shows how long they stayed in the places they went to.

Table 11
Use made of accommodation arranged

Accommodation arranged in	*Length of stay*				
	Did not arrive or failed to stay	*Up to 1 week*	*Over 1 up to 4 weeks*	*Over 4 weeks*	*Total*
After care hostels	5	3	1	3	12
Reception centres	1	2	1	2	6
Common lodging houses/ Emergency shelters	4	1	2	3	10
Hotels, housing associations etc	2	–	2	–	4
Total	12	6	6	8	32

Eleven men failed to arrive at their accommodation and another man refused to stay once he had arrived. Five left before the week they had paid for had expired and one moved on as soon as it did. This left 14 men who chose to stay at their accommodation beyond the initial week. Six left within the first month but eight remained in settled accommodation after four weeks, six of them at the same places, and two, after meeting the requirement of sober attendance at one of the shop fronts run by the Alcoholics Recovery Project, obtained places in a 'dry house' for three weeks.

In terms of settling into accommodation these eight men (one quarter of those placed) can be considered to be 'successes' especially when one considers their past records. Examples of some of these cases follow:

Mick was provisionally found a place in a supportive hostel. He visited the hostel one afternoon prior to release and found it to his satisfaction. Aged 27, he had 14 previous convictions and had been homeless for more than two years. Since release from Pentonville in December 1978, he had lived in Salvation Army hostels, sometimes finding casual work. Although he denied having a drink problem, he said he spent every evening in the pub and occassionally got drunk. Four weeks after release he was still at the hostel and, according to the warden, he was happy there, had a job and had stopped drinking.

Pat, aged 65, had 38 previous convictions and was last released from Pentonville in December 1978. He had had no fixed address for 39 years and in the last year had been in an after-care hostel in Surrey, in common lodging houses in central London, and had also slept rough. He considered he had a drink problem. There were no vacancies at the after care hostel where he had previously stayed, so a place was booked for him in one of the small London reception centres. Six weeks after release Pat was still there and the manager anticipated arranging more suitable accommodation if he so wished. Appointments had been made for him to receive dental attention and to see an optician.

Jack, aged 72, had been NFA for more than 30 years, usually staying in large hostels. He had been a patient in mental hospitals in many parts of the country and had 22 previous convictions. He had 10 previous prison terms, though last released from prison five years ago. On this occasion, according to his own account, he had broken windows in order to be arrested. Jack wanted a place in a Salvation Army hostel but, as he was a 'noisy sleeper', he was not readily accepted by other residents. A special arrangement was made for him to have a separate cubicle where he would not disturb others and he was still at this hostel eight weeks after release and, according to the warden, had not been drunk.

Data about subsequent offending have been collected from two sources, CRO, whence returns were available on 114 cases, and Pentonville's records. Even together these are likely to provide only partial information. Only a small proportion of non-indictable offences are notified to CRO even when these result in prison sentences. Information was gathered about some non-indictable offences from Pentonville's records, including ones for which men were fined and defaulted, but this source would not cover convictions which resulted in being sent to some other establishment.

The period of the follow-up was variable, since the men were released over a three month period, but in general was nine months. For completeness the tables overleaf include the group who rejected actual offers of accommodation but it is so small a group that it would be misleading to place any reliance on its results and so it has been excluded from detailed consideration. Table 12 shows the incidence of having any reconviction and being awarded a further custodial sentence among the men seen during the project, split into categories according to the use they made of its facilities.

Table 12
Rates of reoffending during follow-up period

Requirement category	Total in category about whom information available	Recon-victed		Further prison sentence	
		N	%	N	%
Declined help	54	34	63	25	46
Unable to help	28	19	68	13	46
Placed in accommodation	31	21	68	12	39
Rejected specific offer	(8)	(7)	(88)	(5)	(63)
Total	121	81	68	55	46

Two thirds of the total sample were reconvicted during the follow-up period and, as the table shows, there were no differences between those who did not want help from the project, those it was unable to help and those placed. Slightly fewer of those found accommodation, however, were given new custodial sentences.

Table 13 gives information about the average number of reconvictions, broken down into indictable and non-indictable offences, recorded during the follow-up. Convictions for drunkenness offences are shown in a separate column.

Table 13
Average number of reconvictions for indictable, non-indictable and for drunkenness offences

Requirement category	Total in category about whom information available	All reconvictions	Indictable	Non-indictable excluding drunkenness	Drunken-ness
Declined help	54	1.41	.72	.54	.15
Unable to help	28	1.96	.86	.25	.86
Placed in accommodation	31	1.45	.81	.45	.19
(Rejected specific offer)	(8)	(1.00)	(.75)	(.12)	(.12)
Total	121	1.52	.79	.42	.32

It shows that the group which the project was unable to help had, on average, most reconvictions and that this was due to the very large number (24) of drunkenness convictions they had amassed (seven of which were committed by one individual). The average number of non-indictable offences among the group who declined help was notably boosted by one individual who received 12 such reconvictions.

Information about the average number of custodial sentences, broken down into those for indictable and non-indictable offences, is given in Table 14. (Drunkenness is no longer an imprisonable offence.)

Table 14

Average number of custodial sentences for indictable and non-indictable offences

Requirement category	Total in category about whom information available	Total custodial sentences	:	indictable	non-indictable
Declined help	54	.65		.45	.19
Unable to help	28	.78		.60	.17
Placed in accommodation	31	.50		.44	.06
(Rejected specific offer)	(8)	(.50)		(.50)	(–)
Total	121	.63		.49	.14

Those who were placed in accommodation had fewest custodial sentences. Comparing tables 13 and 14 suggests that they were awarded imprisonment, for indictable and non-indictable offences, relatively less often than either of the other groups. Whether this was attributable to their having settled in the community since release, or to their having a higher level of motivation or to some other factor associated with the project is a matter for speculation. Moreover, this observation has to be treated with some caution because of the bias in the information available, namely that non-indictable offences resulting in a return to Pentonville were recorded in the follow-up study while other such offences were probably missed.

Twelve of those who received no custodial sentences during the follow-up period returned to Pentonville as fine defaulters on remand. Among the whole sample there were 62 instances of imprisonment in Pentonville for non-payment of fines, the majority of them for offences of drunkenness. Those placed in accommodation had 13 fine default periods between them, the group who declined help 20 (this total being inflated by one individual who had eight spells in Pentonville) and the group project was unable to help 28.

It was hoped that the project might enable men to stay out of the criminal justice system for longer than if they had no assistance. However, given the information available, it is difficult to ascertain the extent to which this happened. A comparison between the time men had been at liberty prior to the sentence which brought them into the project and time between release from it and their next conviction (but not necessarily a further imprisonment) shows that at least 11 of those placed in accommodation were longer out of trouble than previously.

Success in terms of avoiding reconviction appears to be related to success in terms of staying in accommodation. Six of the eight men who stayed in accommodation for more than four weeks were not reconvicted during the follow-up period while only two of those who did not arrive at the accommodation stayed out of trouble. The following examples illustrate this point:

John was back in Pentonville four days after release having been sentenced to three months imprisonment for smashing windows (the same offence as his previous one). He had wanted an escort to the hostel where a place had been booked for him but this was not granted and on arrival there he demanded his money back and left. He was aged 36, had been NFA for 16 years, had had 15 previous spells in prison (being last released in September 1978) and had been placed in probation hostels four times, on each occasion breaching his probation order and being sent to prison. In September 1978 he received a further sentence for criminal damage of 12 months imprisonment.

Paddy, aged 59, was an almost continuous resident of Pentonville. The project worker officer described him as 'one of the hard core of recurrent drunks' but arranged for him to go with an escort to a reception centre on release. He stayed there less than a week and ten days after release he appeared in court charged with begging, was fined £5 and was committed immediately to Pentonville for 7 days for non-payment. During the follow-up period he collected a total of seven convictions but only one custodial sentence (one month for theft plus another month for breach of a suspended sentence for shoplifting). He returned to Pentonville four times in all.

James, aged 47, made a promising start. He had been homeless 10 years, and had had an eighteen month period in mental hospital. He considered he had a drink problem and had more than 20 convictions and many spells in prison. He stayed three weeks in a supportive hostel and obtained employment which was unusual for him. His next recorded offence did not' occur until eight months after release, a marked improvement on his previous form when he was sentenced to four months for breaking a window.

Of the three men whose case histories were sketched earlier as examples of those who stayed in their accommodation for longer than four weeks two, Mick and Jack, were not known to have been reconvicted at all during the follow-up period and the other has only one recorded sentence, a fine of £3 for drunkeness which resulted in him spending seven days in Pentonville.

Conclusions

The Pentonville project can be judged from two different standpoints. The first is in terms of whether it provided an acceptable service to homeless persistent petty offenders and the second is in terms of whether it reduced the burden on the criminal justice system.

Consumer satisfaction

Take-up of service was limited in two ways. First, half of the men interviewed either declined help from the outset or rejected a specific arrangement offered to them. Some of these men felt confident that they could find suitable accommodation for themselves, but others found the alternatives offered by the project unacceptable. Second, and more disturbing, another quarter could not be found accommodation by the project, mainly by virtue of their problem drinking and anti-social behaviour. The project officer appeared to have made repeated efforts to persuade men to use his services and had also attempted to secure places even for those with long standing drinking problems who were unacceptable to hostels and common lodging houses. Despite his endeavours only a quarter of those seen during the project were placed in accommodation. These results indicate that more alternatives need to be offered at the higher end of the range of provision to attract a greater proportion to use the service, and that, at the lower end, more resources are needed in order to cope with the problems of the group rejected by existing facilities.

Not all of those placed can be considered satisfied customers. Eleven of the 32 men placed failed to arrive at their accommodation even though, in the majority of cases, they had already paid one week's rent. This suggests firstly that more should be done to raise motivation and confidence prior to release. Initially there was resistance on the part of the project officer to involve the volunteers and so their full potential in this respect was not explored during the study. Particularly, the idea of escorting prisoners to their accommodation was not properly tested and, given the large number of men who failed to arrive, it appears that some men should have been more strongly persuaded to accept this service. Secondly, however, the results perhaps indicate dissatisfaction with the accommodation arranged. This is further borne out by the fact that of the 21 who actually arrived, a third failed to stay for the week they had paid for. Some men are known to have been forced to leave after breaking rules or drinking excessively but others simply left and did not return. This may have been due in part to the facilities not fitting expectations which may have been raised by the project. A volunteer who escorted one man to a reception centre described her impressions of the atmosphere:

> The decor and whole ambience of the place was very much the same as Pentonville itself but none of the doors had locks and no resident had any privacy. If this is all a man can be offered there is not much incentive for him to keep out of prison, for he is not much better off outside. There was nothing about (the centre) which could be even remotely termed as 'home' for any one.

She added that she was not suprised to discover that the man she had escorted had got drunk the first night and left the hostel after a few days. Ideally facilities that can be treated as homes rather than as shelters should be available. This seems to call for many small units rather than the huge institutions that are currently used. However the project did appear to provide a satisfactory service to some residents. Thirteen of the 32 men placed stayed at their accommodation beyond the initial week and eight remained beyond four weeks.

Relieving the criminal justice system

The numbers included in the project were small so it would be misleading to place much reliance on its findings regarding subsequent criminality. However, although an equally large proportion among those placed in accommodation as among the rest of those covered by the project were reconvicted in the ensuing nine months, slightly fewer of them were subsequently awarded prison sentences. To this extent at least, the project may have reduced the potential load on the criminal justice system which was the primary aim of the project. Moreover, a third of the group who found accommodation kept out of the criminal justice system for periods longer than their previous periods at liberty from prison and six of the eight men who stayed for more than four weeks in their accommodation were not reconvicted at all during the follow-up period.

Given the difficulties of working with this group and of having any impact on their behaviour even the small achievements demonstrated by this project are noteworthy. The results indicate that there may be some advantages both to some homeless persistent petty offenders and to the criminal justice system from providing an accommodation service at the point of release from prison. While they suggest that there is a need to strengthen the service by widening the range of resources available and providing greater support to help the men to avail themselves of the opportunities offered, they justify the efforts put into the Pentonville project. It is therefore encouraging that, since the experimental project ended, the work of the project has been continued by the welfare liaison unit in Pentonville as part of its regular workload, and the service is now potentially available to a wider group comprising all those in prison for three months or less (except those serving only a few days) including fine defaulters and civil prisoners.

6 Helping socially isolated prisoners

by John Corden and Maggie Clifton

Background

In 1976 The Home Office made a grant to the University of York to support a survey of the experiences of men leaving prison who were not subject to parole or any other form of statutory licence. This survey identified certain factors which were associated with decisions by prisoners to seek help after release through the voluntary after-care provided by the probation service. The original hypothesis had been that those men with strong informal networks of relatives and friends would be less likely to seek help from the probation and after-care service than more isolated men. Although the survey produced some evidence to support this hypothesis, it also revealed the existence of a number of extremely isolated men who were less likely than well-supported or moderately isolated men to take the initiative in making contact with the probation service on release from prison (Corden J. *et al.*, 1978, p. 71).

A number of possible explanations for this finding were proposed: these included the possibility that isolated men avoided social interaction of any kind whenever they could; the idea that they saw their own situation as hopeless, and therefore not worth attempting to change; and the possibility that the probation service did not offer the kind of help which met their immediate needs. It was also suggested that because their situations seemed hopeless and depressing, or because developments in penal policy accorded such men a low priority, the service might not make great efforts to encourage such men to seek their help and might sometimes act in ways which reinforced the beliefs of isolated men that their situations were hopeless and not worth bothering with (Corden J. *et al.*, 1980, p. 85).

The very low rate of take-up of voluntary after-care by this group was worrying for a number of reasons: first, the most isolated men had, in many cases, acute problems of homelessness which were made worse by their imprisonment; second, isolated men tended to end up in prison for less serious offences, presumably because the courts were more reluctant to consider alternatives, such as fines, or – when they did – the men were less able to fulfil the requirements of non-custodial penalties; and third, because another study has suggested that petty short-term prisoners who are homeless are highly likely to return to prison (Banks & Fairhead, 1976, p. 17). It seemed that this group of men provided an opportunity, not at present fully exploited, for probation officers to concentrate on giving help and alleviating immediate needs in ways which might also result in reductions of the pressure on the prison population.

In the report published after the results of this survey were analysed, a number of recommendations and proposals were made. One of these was that the probation service in Leeds should adopt an experimental strategy of deliberately reaching-out to the most isolated prisoners and that the implementation of this strategy should be monitored both to see whether this approach would significantly increase the take-up of voluntary after-care amongst this vulnerable group, and to assess whether this kind of action by probation officers could lead to any significant changes in prisoners' post-release situations (Corden J. *et al.*, 1978, p. 80).

The socially isolated prisoners' project
This proposal was taken up by the West Yorkshire probation and after-care service which was granted funds to appoint three ancillary workers out of the £600,000 windfall allocated to the service in the April 1978 budget. Manpower constraints imposed by the Home Office prevented the service from spending this money on increasing the numbers of qualified probation officers, but the appointment of ancillary staff was not forbidden. These workers were appointed early in 1979, and took up their posts in April, to form the socially isolated prisoners' project.

The project aims to offer a service to men coming out of Armley and Rudgate prisons into Leeds who are not subject to any form of statutory licence. Prison welfare officers in these two prisons have been asked to notify the project of any men being released into Leeds who were homeless or living alone before arrest, or who expect to be in either of these positions on release. All men who are notified to the project are visited before release by one of the ancillaries, unless they are found to be on a probation officer's caseload in which case the service is only offered after consultation with the officer concerned.

In the pre-release visit, the ancillaries introduce themselves and explain the origins of the project before going on to discuss the man's post-release plans and any difficulties he expects to encounter. Except where it becomes clear that any offer of help would be inappropriate, the ancillaries then go on to offer to meet the man at the prison gate on his release, and to accompany him on his visits to social security offices, landlords and/or hostels, and on any initiatives he wishes to take in relation to employment. Some men prefer not to be met in which case they are invited to come to the project office as soon as they reach the centre of Leeds. Where a man's immediate practical problems are not resolved by the end of the day of release, he may be invited to return on the following day to finish off these tasks.

The ancillaries also try to work closely with probation officers where they are involved in a case, and to introduce men to probation officers at some time during the day, or later, where there is a clear indication either that the man would welcome some contact over a longer period, or where he has problems which seem to require the skill, status, or authority of a trained probation officer – for example, men who are seeking help with alcohol problems or interpersonal difficulties are usually referred on, as are men who are due to appear in court again or are seeking an advocate for their cause with the housing department.

The ancillaries do not have access to any special resources; there is no accommodation or landladies' scheme, nor any special employment-finding project run by the probation service in Leeds. By dint of accompanying a substantial number of men through Department of Health and Social Security offices and other agencies, they have established a basis of trust with many counter-staff, which helps to smooth the path for some of their clients, but the main emphasis has been on helping men to negotiate the best arrangement they can for themselves, by keeping them company, providing transport, offering corroboration, and helping to bolster morale, rather than by doing things for them and providing 'ready-made' solutions.

Research into the project
Research into the impact of the project is being carried out by the Department of Social Administration and Social Work at the University of York, supported by a grant from the Home Office. Four main areas are being explored. The first is to assess how a reaching-out strategy is received by socially isolated men, and whether they accept the offer of help significantly more often than if they had been left to seek it of their own initiative. The second is to assess to what extent, if at all, this intervention reduces the difficulties which some men experienced in obtaining an income and a place to live shown in the previous study. The third area which it is hoped to examine is the extent to which this work on the day of release, focussed on a man's immediate practical needs, has any longer-term spin-offs, such as a reduced rate of reconviction, or the establishment of a longer-term relationship with a probation officer. Finally, we hope to explore the relationship between this special project and the probation service in the area.

Initial stages of the project
A number of difficulties have been encountered in the course of the first year of the project. Notification of eligible prisoners is the responsibility of prison welfare officers in the two prisons concerned. For them, a special project in Leeds was just one of a wide range of resources with which they were expected to be familiar in towns and cities throughout Yorkshire and beyond; it was not suprising that they did not immediately begin to refer all those who fitted the criteria. In some instances, they used their discretion to assess whether a man would accept or benefit from notification to the project, and in other cases they did not immediately grasp the criteria for notification. In recent months the rate of notifications has improved.

There is considerable fluctuation in the rates of discharge of isolated prisoners from Armley and Rudgate, as a result of such diverse factors as summer holidays in the fines and fees office, and the levels of overcrowding within the prisons. This has meant that the workload falling on the project varies considerably with all the attendant consequences for morale which this entails. Even after men are notified, and occasionally after the pre-release visit, men are transferred out to prisons where the service cannot be offered. A few men are released a day or two earlier than originally planned, while others are re-arrested at the gate.

The scarcity of private, rented accommodation in Leeds is such that even a fairly intensive search through the day may not reveal any accommodation which can be secured with the money available to a prisoner either from his discharge grant or his social security entitlement. This problem is exacerbated by the absence of many landlords during the day, so that negotiations cannot even begin until after Department of Health and Social Security offices are shut. Men are often faced with the choice of booking a place in the local authority men's hostel while there is still room, or running the risk of being left homeless, and therefore in some cases penniless, at the end of the day, in the uncertain hope of securing the tenancy of a furnished room.

Men who are not entitled to any discharge grant form a substantial proportion of those notified to the project, and they have to spend a considerable part of the day attending the Department of Health and Social Security offices to obtain money to pay for accommodation. They cannot obtain money until they have an address, although a provisional booking at the local authority men's hostel which is corroborated by the ancillary will suffice. The time spent at the Department of Health and Social Security severely restricts the amount of time which can be devoted to a search for accommodation.

Some of these problems can be influenced by the project or probation management but others are quite beyond their control. Nevertheless, the indications so far are that a substantial number of men who are offered help accept it. In the first 9 months the offer to be met at the gate was accepted in 53 out of 91 cases, and in a further 8 cases the men expressed a preference for getting to the office under their own steam and carried out that intention. All those men who stayed with the ancillaries throughout the day had some accommodation and an income by the end of the day, albeit some of these would have preferred a higher or more private and secure standard of accommodation than was actually achieved. In a few cases, men have made substantial progress in the search for employment on the day of release. In some cases other problems have also been tackled – suitable clothing has been provided, health problems have been confronted and men have been introduced to probation officers.

It is too early to evaluate the project in a comprehensive way, but there is some evidence that isolated men respond positively to a reaching-out strategy directed to their immediate needs. With additional resources, particularly in relation to private furnished accommodation, the immediate impact of the project could be even more favourable.

7 Conclusions

Social control versus welfare provision
In Chapter 1 it was noted that two considerations had to be taken into account in deciding whether alternatives to prison could be used for some cases, namely public safety and justice. The subsequent research has tended to show, however, that other factors influence decisions about arresting and sentencing petty offenders, with the result that some individuals are more liable to be arrested and sent to prison because of their social circumstances rather than through reference to either of those requirements.

The persistent petty offenders studied had committed two distinct types of offence, although in practice many of them had both types in their records. The first category is of crimes which can be considered victimless, such as drunkeness or wandering abroad (this category can be extended to cover begging which, although it may cause nuisance or affront to people, cannot be said to cause physical harm). The second is of crimes against the property or persons of others, such as theft, criminal damage and assault. However, because the research was concerned with a group defined to be at the extreme end of the scale in terms of criminality, these offences, though often repeated, were typically trivial, committed on the spur of the moment and involving little serious or lasting harm.

Offences in the first category cannot be said to prejudice public safety and, although they cause nuisance, disquiet and discomfort to the community, cannot justify sending individuals to prison, thereby incurring substantial public expenditure. Offences in the second category are not to be dismissed lightly, but the interests of justice are not well served by using imprisonment; a penalty that should perhaps be reserved for serious offences and ones that deserve public condemnation.

It is partly because they are persistent nuisances that the courts resort to imprisoning these offenders, in a desire to give themselves, the police and the public a rest. However, the research also indicated that concern for the welfare of the offender also contributed to decisions in respect of members of this group, both at the point of arrest and at that of sentence, such that some decisions were a response to the lack of alternative provision appropriate to individuals' needs and circumstances.

Welfare services which are normally provided by social services departments, hospitals, housing authorities etc often appear beyond the reach of this group of people, either because these agencies lack relevant facilities or are unwilling to grant access to a group who are troublesome or unrewarding to work with, or because the individuals themselves have rejected the help available. In these circumstances the criminal justice system appears to act as the agency of last resort for those whose needs fail to be met through the usual channels. Thus, the police arrest and charge individuals whom they perceive as in need of care and attention in order to provide them with shelter, food or medical attention, and magistrates are influenced in their sentencing decisions by the same considerations, and will award custodial sentences or periods of remand in custody as a rest cure. (Archard (1975) also noted this phenomenon). The individuals concerned may also exploit the system, committing offences in order to get a respite from the hardships they face. For example, Prewer (1959) found that among his sample of persons in prison for smashing windows some men had the deliberate intention of being sent to prison for shelter and other comforts.

This confusion of function is not efficient, in that it results in persons whose nuisance behaviour hardly warrants attention being brought into the criminal justice system. Neither, as noted above, is it just in that it leads to a disadvantaged group being subjected to some degree of punishment and limitations on their freedom, in order that their needs be met. Nor is it beneficial to the individuals selected for 'help'. Experience of the criminal justice system invariably serves to consolidate the original disadvantage, since it is more difficult to find accommodation and employment or to re-establish contact with family and friends after a prison sentence than before (cf. Fairhead, 1978). In order for alternative decisions to be made, therefore, welfare provision that is, as far as feasible, separate from the controlling and punitive function of the criminal justice system is required.

Provision to facilitate alternative decisions
The research to date has helped to identify and clarify certain needs and has suggested that two specific facilities be developed in order to keep persistent petty offenders out of prison. Further research will, however, be needed to show whether these particular facilities will be used and will be effective.

The first of these facilities, shelters to which the police could escort persons they would otherwise arrest and charge for offences of drunkenness, would keep individuals out of the criminal justice system altogether, and to the extent that they gave access to welfare provision this would also be outside that system. Simple overnight shelters from which drunks would be discharged once they had sobered up would only provide very rudimentary services on the spot, limited to first aid. They could however act as referral points to existing facilities provided by the statutory and voluntary agencies, whose services currently are not utilised by this group for the reasons noted above. It is hoped that by developing the second provision, day centres, the courts may be able to keep in the community offenders they might otherwise have sent to prison. There are various possible ways in which day centres can meet the court's requirements

70

that offenders be supervised. There are some instances in which attendance at the centre is a specific condition written into the probation order at the time sentence is passed, in cases where the offender would otherwise have been sentenced to imprisonment. In cases where the offender would not have faced a custodial sentence a less formal type of requirement to attend the centre is being used consisting of a contract agreed between individuals on probation and their supervising officer.

Many existing day centres, including some run by the probation and after-care service and others run by the voluntary agencies, operate at a much more informal level and are run as drop-in centres. Such centres provide a place where people may go to find companionship, a place to sit to talk, read the newspaper or play cards, and obtain cheap or free refreshment. They therefore fill pressing needs of the homeless, and some of them are indeed already used by the 'hard core' of persistent petty offenders. Even though these centres make no specific demands on their users, they can still enable an individual to comply with a probation order simply by providing somewhere where an officer and his client can meet and establish an acceptable relationship. Moreover, by giving the homeless somewhere to go that takes them off the street and away from public attention, such day centres may enable them to avoid arrest and reconviction, and may actually reduce the nuisance caused by this group. The existence of a day centre can make more credible the use of the conditional discharge as an alternative to fining homeless offenders who lack means to pay and therefore end up in prison for default.

Another role for day centres is to co-ordinate resources for their users. Day centres are likely to attract individuals whose needs, for accommodation, medical attention, help with drink problems etc. are not being attended to and therefore ought to build up a network of contacts and resources to which they can make appropriate referrals.

Access to facilities
New resources, such as those described above, are also appropriate for people who suffer similar disadvantages without ever falling foul of the police and courts. The question therefore arises of whether there should be open access to these facilities. There are two strong reasons for making them available to all who wish to make use of them. Firstly, where facilities are provided that are restricted to offenders or to certain groups of offenders then individuals who wish to use them may contrive to gain admittance to them by committing appropriate offences. Thus the burden on the criminal justice system may increase rather than decrease if desirable facilities have restricted entry. The second argument is about equity. As noted in Chapter 1, and illustrated in Chapter 3, the results of decision-making at the point of arrest are not always entirely equitable, particularly in respect of the most trivial offending where there is widest scope for discretion. Thus, it would be unfair if some individuals were to qualify for preferential treatment because they have been apprehended

71

while others whose circumstances were similar were overlooked. Given these considerations, the further question of whether such facilities should be provided inside or outside the criminal justice system arises.

Predicting demand

It was hoped that the research would provide a basis for estimating the scale on which new resources would need to be provided. However, there are difficulties about predicting demand for new facilities relying on information available prior to them being available. Current decisions are made on the basis of the current system and not all the consequences of changing the system to allow alternative decisions can necessarily be forseen in advance. For example, if the police are given an alternative to arrest homeless drunks (by the provision of shelters where the drunks can sober up) they may not only divert the drunks they used to arrest, but, if they see the facility as offering a positive service, they may initiate more contacts with homeless persons and make more use of the shelters than could be predicted from current arrest figures. Estimating demand is also made more complicated if access is to be open to anybody who wishes to use the facility.

Predicting the impact on the prison population

It is also difficult to predict the effect on the prison population of establishing new facilities of the two types discussed, because their impact would largely be indirect. The provision of shelters to which the police could escort drunks would effect savings by reducing the number of persons received into prison for non-payment or fines for drunkenness offences.

Day centres could have a direct impact on the number being sentenced to imprisonment and also various indirect ones. They might enable more offenders to comply with probation orders (thus avoiding imprisonment for breaching their conditions) and might influence magistrates to impose fewer fines on those lacking means. Moreover, by providing a refuge away from public attention, day centres may help prevent homeless individuals falling foul of the law.

As the absolute numbers of older persistent petty offenders among those sentenced to imprisonment is small, the main contribution in terms of relieving prison overcrowding to be achieved by setting up these facilities will be in reducing the number of fine defaulters received into local prisons. However, even if such new provision constitutes an effective intervention and does substantially reduce the number of persistent petty offenders in prison, the impact will not be sufficient to solve the current problem of the excess size of the prison population, as the group that has been identified is too small. Additional remedies, such as those mentioned at the beginning of Chapter 1 (awarding shorter sentences to all those imprisoned; increasing remission or granting more parole) will have to be sought.

This research has, however, indicated that some persistent petty offenders return frequently to prison because of their social circumstances rather than because they pose any threat to society. In the interests of equity, justice and efficiency, all possible efforts should be devoted to keeping such individuals out of prison and where possible out of the criminal justice system altogether. In order to achieve this it is important to consider whether their welfare needs can be met adequately through the criminal justice system or need to be met independently of it, so that decisions about arresting and sentencing are based solely on universally applicable considerations about social control and justice.

References

Archard, P. (1975). *The Bottle Won't Leave You: a study of homeless alcoholics and their guardians*. London: Alcoholics Recovery Project.

Banks, C. and Fairhead, S. (1976). *The Petty Short-Term Prisoner*. Chichester: Howard League and Barry Rose.

Barnard, E. and Bottoms, A. E. (1979). 'Facilitating decisions not to imprison' in *The Persistent Petty Offender*. London: NACRO.

Corden, J., Kuipers, J. and Wilson, A. K. (1978). *After Prison: the post release experiences of discharged prisoners*. Papers in Community Studies, No. 21, Department of Social Administration and Social Work, University of York.

Corden, J., Kuipers, J. and Wilson, A. K. (1980). 'Prison welfare and voluntary after-care'. *British Journal of Social Work*, Vol. 10, No. 1, pp. 71-86.

Fairhead, S. (1978). 'The vagrant and the criminal justice system'. *Justice of the Peace*, Vol. 142, No. 40, pp. 584-585.

Fairhead, S. and Marshall, T. F. (1979). 'Dealing with the petty persistent offender' in *The Persistent Petty Offender*. London: NACRO.

Home Office. (1978). 'A survey of the south-east prison population'. *Home Office Research Bulletin*, No. 5, pp. 12–24.

Home Office. Annual. *Criminal Statistics, England and Wales*, London: HMSO.

Prewer, R. R. (1959). 'Some observations on window smashing'. *British Journal of Delinquency*, Vol. 10, pp. 104-13.

Publications

Titles already published for the Home Office

Postage extra

Studies in the Causes of Delinquency and the Treatment of Offenders

1. Prediction methods in relation to borstal training. Hermann Mannheim and Leslie T. Wilkins. 1955. vi+276pp. (11 340051 9) £3.

2. †Time spent awaiting trial. Evelyn Gibson. 1960. 46pp. (34-368-2) 27p.

3. †Delinquent generations. Leslie T. Wilkins. 1960. 20pp. (11 340053 5) 16p.

4. Murder. Evelyn Gibson and S. Klein. 1961. 44pp. (11 340054 3) 30p.

5. Persistent criminals. A study of all offenders liable to preventive detention in 1956. W. H. Hammond and Edna Chayen. 1963. x+238pp. (34-368-5) £1.25.

6. Some statistical and other numerical techniques for classifying individuals. P. Mc-Naughton-Smith. 1965. 34pp. (34-368-6) 17½p.

7. Probation research: a preliminary report. Part I. General outline of research. Part II. Study of Middlesex probation area (SOMPA). Steven Folkard, Kate Lyon, Margaret M. Carver and Erica O'Leary. 1966. vi+58pp. (11 340374 7) 42p.

8. †Probation research: national study of probation. Trends and regional comparisons in probation (England and Wales). Hugh Barr and Erica O'Leary. 1966. viii+52pp. (34-368-8) 25p.

9. †Probation research. A survey of group work in the probation service. Hugh Barr. 1966. viii+96pp. (34-368-9) 40p.

10. †Types of delinquency and home background. A validation study of Hewitt and Jenkins' hypothesis. Elizabeth Field. 1967. vi+22pp. (34-368-10) 14p.

11. †Studies of female offenders. No. 1—Girls of 16 – 20 years sentenced to borstal or detention centre training in 1963. No. 2—Women offenders in the Metropolitan Police District in March and April 1957. No. 3—A description of women in prison on January 1, 1965. Nancy Goodman and Jean Price. 1967. vi+78pp. (34-368-11) 30p.

12. †The use of the Jesness Inventory on a sample of British probationers. Martin Davies. 1967. iv+20pp. (34-368-12) 11p.

13. The Jesness Inventory: application to approved school boys. Joy Mott. 1969. iv+28pp. (11 340063 2) 17½p.

Home Office Research Studies

1. Workloads in children's departments. Eleanor Grey. 1969. vi+75pp. (11 340101 9) 37½p.

2. †Probationers in their social environment. A study of male probationers aged 17 – 20, together with an analysis of those reconvicted within twelve months. Martin Davies. 1969. vii+204pp. (11 340102 7) 87½p.

---

†Out of print. Photostat copies can be purchased from Her Majesty's Stationery Office upon request.

3. Murder 1957 to 1968. A Home Office Statistical Division report on murder in England and Wales. Evelyn Gibson and S. Klein (with annex by the Scottish Home and Health Department on murder in Scotland). 1969. vi+94pp. (11 340103 5) 60p.

4. Firearms in crime. A Home Office Statistical Division report on indictable offences involving firearms in England and Wales. A. D. Weatherhead and B. M. Robinson. 1970. viii+37pp. (11 340104 3) 30p.

5. †Financial penalties and probation. Martin Davies. 1970. vii+38pp. (11 340105 1) 30p.

6. Hostels for probationers. Study of the aims, working and variations in the effectiveness of male probation hostels with special reference to the influence of the environment on delinquency. Ian Sinclair. 1971. iv+199pp. (11 340106 X) £1.15.

7. Prediction methods in criminology including a prediction study of young men on probation. Frances H. Simon. 1971. xi+233pp. (11 340107 8) £1.25.

8. †Study of the juvenile liason scheme in West Ham 1961 – 1965. Marilyn Taylor. 1971. vi+45pp. (11 340108 6) 35p.

9. Explorations in after-care. I—After-care units in London, Liverpool and Manchester. Martin Silberman (Royal London Prisoners' Aid Society), Brenda Chapman. II — After-care hostels receiving a Home Office grant. Ian Sinclair and David Snow (HORU). III—St Martin of Tours House, Aryeh Leissner (National Bureau for Co-operation in Child Care). 1971. xi+168pp. (11 340109 4) 85p.

10. A survey of adoption in Great Britain. Eleanor Grey in collaboration with R. M. Blunden. 1971. ix+168pp. (11 340110 8) 95p.

11. †Thirteen-year-old approved school boys in 1962. Elizabeth Field, W. H. Hammond and J. Tizard. 1971. ix+45pp. (11 340111 6) 35p.

12. Absconding from approved schools. R. V. G. Clarke and D. N. Martin. 1971. vi+145pp. (11 340112 4) 85p.

13. An experiment in personality assessment of young men remanded in custody. H. Sylvia Anthony. 1972. viii+79pp. (11 340113 2) 52½p.

14. Girl offenders aged 17 – 20 years. I—Statistics relating to girl offenders aged 17 – 20 years from 1960 to 1970. II—Re-offending by girls released from borstal or detention centre training. III—The problems of girls released from borstal training during their period on after-care. Jean Davies and Nancy Goodman. 1972. v+77pp. (11 340114 0) 52½p.

15. †The controlled trial in institutional research—paradigm or pitfall for penal evaluators? R. V. G. Clarke and D. B. Cornish. 1972. v+33pp. (11 340115 9) 29p.

16. A survey of fine enforcement. Paul Softley. 1973. v+65pp. (11 340116 7) 47p.

17. †An index of social environment designed for use in social work research. Martin Davies. 1973. v+61pp. (11 340117 5) 47p.

18. †Social enquiry reports and the probation service. Martin Davies and Andrea Knopf. 1973. v+47pp. (11 340118 3) 50p.

19. †Depression, psychopathic personality and attempted suicide in a borstal sample. H. Sylvia Anthony. 1973. viii+44pp. (0 11 340119 1) 36½p.

20. The use of bail and custody by London magistrates' courts before and after the Criminal Justice Act 1967. Frances Simon and Mollie Weatheritt. 1974. vi+78pp. (0 11 340120 5) 57p.

21. Social work in the environment. A study of one aspect of probation practice. Martin Davies, with Margaret Rayfield, Alaster Calder and Tony Fowles. 1974. x+164pp. (0 11 340121 3) £1.10.

22. Social work in prisons. An experiment in the use of extended contact with offenders. Margaret Shaw. 1974. viii+156pp. (0 11 340122 1) £1.45.

23. Delinquency amongst opiate users. Joy Mott and Marilyn Taylor. 1974. vi+54pp. (0 11 340663 0) 41p.

---

†Out of print. Photostat copies can be purchased from Her Majesty's Stationery Office upon request.

24. IMPACT. Intensive matched probation and after-care treatment. Vol. 1. The design of the probation experiment and an interim evaluation. M. S. Folkard, A. J. Fowles, B. C. McWilliams, W. McWilliams, D. D. Smith, D. E. Smith and G. R. Walmsley. 1974. vi+54pp. (0 11 340664 9) £1.25.

25. The approved school experience. An account of boys' experience of training under differing regimes of approved schools, with an attempt to evaluate the effectiveness of that training. Anne B. Dunlop. 1974. viii+124pp. (0 11 340665 7). £1.22.

26. Absconding from open prisons. Charlotte Banks, Patricia Mayhew and R. J. Sapsford. 1975. viii+92pp. (0 11 340666 5) 95p.

27. Driving while disqualified. Sue Kriefman. 1975. vi+138pp. (0 11 340667 3) £1.22.

28. Some male offenders' problems. I—Homeless offenders in Liverpool. W. McWilliams. II—Casework with short-term prisoners. Julie Holborn. 1975. x+150pp. (0 11 340668 1) £2.50.

29. Community service orders. K. Pease, P. Durkin. I. Earnshaw, D. Payne and J. Thorpe. 1975. viii+80pp. (0 11 340669 X) 75p.

30. Field Wing Bail Hostel: the first nine months. Frances Simon and Sheena Wilson. 1975. viii+56pp. (0 11 340670 3) 85p.

31. Homicide in England and Wales 1967 – 1971. Evelyn Gibson. 1975. iv+60pp. (0 11 340753 X) 90p.

32. Residential treatment and its effects on delinquency. D. B. Cornish and R. V. G. Clarke. 1975. vi+74pp. (0 11 340672 X) £1.00.

33. Further studies of female offenders. Part A: Borstal girls eight years after release. Nancy Goodman, Elizabeth Maloney and Jean Davies. Part B: The sentencing of women at the London Higher Courts. Nancy Goodman, Paul Durkin and Janet Halton. Part C: Girls appearing before a juvenile court. Jean Davies. 1976. vi+114pp. (0 11 340673 8) £1.55.

34. Crime as opportunity. P. Mayhew, R. V. G. Clarke, A. Sturman and J. M. Hough. 1976. vii+36pp. (0 11 340674 6) 70p.

35. The effectiveness of sentencing: a review of the literature. S. R. Brody. 1976. v+89pp. (0 11 340675 4) £1.15.

36. IMPACT. Intensive matched probation and after-care treatment. Vol. II—The results of the experiment. M. S. Folkard, D. E. Smith and D. D. Smith. 1976. xi+40pp. (0 11 340676 2) 80p.

37. Police cautioning in England and Wales. J. A. Ditchfield. 1976. iv+31pp. (0 11 340677 0) 65p.

38. Parole in England and Wales. C. P. Nuttall, with E. E. Barnard, A. J. Fowles, A. Frost, W. H. Hammond, P. Mayhew, K. Pease, R. Tarling and M. J. Weatheritt. 1977. vi+90pp. (0 11 340678 9) £1.75.

39. Community service assessed in 1976. K. Pease, S. Billingham and I. Earnshaw. 1977. vi+29pp. (0 11 340679 7) 75p.

40. Screen violence and film censorship. Stephen Brody. 1977. vi+179pp. (0 11 340680 0) £2.75.

41. Absconding from borstals. Gloria K. Laycock. 1977. v+82pp. (0 11 340681 9) £1.50.

42. Gambling—a review of the literature and its implications for policy and research. D. B. Cornish. 1978. xii+284pp. (0 11 340682 7) £4.25.

43. Compensation orders in magistrates' courts. Paul Softley. 1978. vi+41pp. (0 11 340683 5) 90p.

44. Research in criminal justice. John Croft. 1978. vi+16pp. (0 11 340684 3) 50p.

45. Prison welfare: an account of an experiment at Liverpool. A. J. Fowles. 1978. v+34pp. (0 11 340685 1) 75p.

46. Fines in magistrates' courts. Paul Softley. 1978. v+42pp. (0 11 340686 X) £1.00.

47. Tackling vandalism. R. V. G. Clarke (editor), F. J. Gladstone, A. Sturman and Sheena Wilson (contributors). 1978. vi+91pp. (0 11 340687 8) £2.00.

48. Social inquiry reports: a survey. Jennifer Thorpe. 1979. vi+55pp. (0 11 340688 6) £1.50.
49. Crime in public view. P. Mayhew, R. V. G. Clarke, J. N. Burrows, J. M. Hough and S. W. C. Winchester. 1979. v+36pp. (0 11 340689 4) £1.00.
50. Crime and the community. John Croft. 1979. v+16pp. (0 11 340690 8) 65p.
51. Life-sentence prisoners. David Smith (editor), Christopher Brown, Joan Worth, Roger Sapsford and Charlotte Banks (contributors). 1979. v+52pp. (0 11 340691 6) £1.25.
52. Hostels for offenders. Jane E. Andrews with an appendix by Bill Sheppard. 1979. v+30pp. (0 11 340692 4) £1.50.
53. Previous convictions, sentence and reconviction: a statistical study of a sample of 5,000 offenders convicted in January 1971. G. J. O. Phillpotts and L. B. Lancucki. 1979. v+55pp. (0 11 340693 2) £2.25.
54. Sexual offences, consent and sentencing. Roy Walmsley and Karen White. 1979. vi+77pp. (0 11 340694 0) £2.75.
55. Crime prevention and the police. John Burrows, Paul Ekblom and Kevin Heal. 1979. v+37pp. (0 11 340695 9) £1.75.
56. Sentencing practice in magistrates' courts. Roger Tarling with the assistance of Mollie Weatheritt. 1979. vii+54pp. (0 11 340696 7) £2.25.
57. Crime and comparative research. John Croft. 1979. iv+16pp. (0 11 340697 5) £1.00.
58. Race, crime and arrests. Philip Stevens and Carole F. Willis. 1979. v+69pp. (0 11 340698 3) £2.75.
59. Research and criminal policy. John Croft. 1980. iv+14pp. (0 11 340699 1) £1.75.
60. Junior attendance centres. Anne B. Dunlop. 1980. v+47pp. (0 11 340700 9) £2.75.
61. Police interrogation: an observational study in four police stations. Paul Softley with the assistance of David Brown, Bob Forde, George Mair and David Moxon. 1980. vii+67pp. (0 11 340701 7) £3.90.
62. Co-ordinating crime prevention efforts. F. J. Gladstone. 1980. v+74pp. (0 11 340702 5) £3.90.
63. Crime prevention publicity: an assessment. D. Riley and P. Mayhew. 1980. v+47pp. (0 11 340703 3) £3.30.
64. Taking offenders out of circulation. Stephen Brody and Roger Tarling. 1980. v+46pp. (0 11 340704 1) £3.00.
65. Alcoholism and social policy: are we on the right lines? Mary Tuck. 1980. v+30pp. (0 11 340705 X) £2.70.

HMSO
The above publications can be purchased from the Government Bookshops at the addresses listed on cover page iv (post orders to PO Box 569, London SE1 9NH) or through booksellers.

The following Home Office research publications are available on request from the Home Office Research Unit, Information Section, 50 Queen Anne's Gate, London, SW1H 9AT.

Research Unit Papers
1. Uniformed police work and management technology. J. M. Hough. 1980.
2. Supplementary information on sexual offences and sentencing. Roy Walmsley and Karen White. 1980.

Research Bulletin
The Research Bulletin is published twice a year and consists mainly of short articles relating to projects which are part of the Home Office Research Unit's research programme.

Printed in Wales for Her Majesty's Stationery Office by CSP Printing of Cardiff
Dd 716559 K14 1/81